D0498467

THE HISTORY OF
LITTLE ORPHAN ANNIE

The History of Little Orphan Annie

BRUCE SMITH

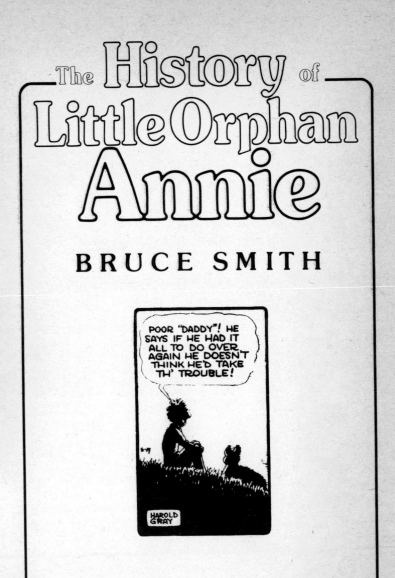

POOR "DADDY"! HE SAYS IF HE HAD IT ALL TO DO OVER AGAIN HE DOESN'T THINK HE'D TAKE TH' TROUBLE!

HAROLD GRAY

BALLANTINE BOOKS · NEW YORK

The author is grateful to:

Special Collections, Mugar Memorial Library, Boston University, for permission to quote from Harold Gray's letters and to reproduce the photograph of Harold Gray, the original *Little Orphan Annie* comic strips showing Mrs. Oliver Warbucks taking Annie home, Oliver Warbucks arriving home to find Annie, the illustrations of Annie replying to frequently asked questions, Daddy Warbucks going off on mysterious trips, the first time Daddy went away, Mrs. Warbucks sending Annie back to the home, the photo of Mitzi Green, the strips demonstrating Daddy Warbucks as Gray's "alter ego," and the Junior Commando movement poster; the New York *Daily News* for permission to reproduce the photo of Joseph Medill Patterson, and the first *Little Orphan Annie* Sunday comic strip; the Tribune Company Syndicate for providing all other comic strips of *Little Orphan Annie,* including those drawn by Leonard Starr; Richard Marschall for the two Little Orphan Annie song covers, the advertisement aimed at newspaper editors, Harold and Winifred Gray's Christmas cards, and the Annie, Daddy, and Sandy portrait that hung in the offices of the Tribune Syndicate; WGN, Chicago, for the photo of the cast of the *Little Orphan Annie* radio show with Shirley Bell; Ovaltine for the photo of its promotional mugs; Capp Enterprises for the spoof in *Li'l Abner* (copyright 1982, Capp Enterprises, Inc.); *Mad* Magazine for the caricature of Annie as all grown up (copyright 1960 by E. C. Publications, Inc.); *Playboy* Magazine for the picture of Little Annie Fanny; David Powers for the photo of Strouse, Charnin, and Meehan, and the advertisement for the Broadway show *Annie*; Leonard Starr for his earlier strip *On Stage*; Columbia Pictures/Rastar for the photos from the movie *Annie*; and Columbia Pictures Merchandising for the photo of Annie products it licenses.

Library of Congress Catalog Card Number: 82-90027

ISBN: 0-345-30546-9

A NEW MARKET BOOK PROJECT

Manufactured in the United States of America

First Edition: June 1982

10 9 8 7 6 5 4 3 2 1

CONTENTS

Foreword by Worth Gatewood vii

Chapter 1   ONLY AN ORPHAN 1

Chapter 2   "THE KID LOOKS LIKE A PANSY TO ME" 6

Chapter 3   HARD TIMES 22

Chapter 4   THAT LITTLE CHATTERBOX

Chapter 5   "WE'RE DOIN' *WAR* WORK" 46

Chapter 6   "WHAT A GIRL!" 64

Chapter 7   "ANNIE WILL BE MISSED" 82

Chapter 8   "THE WORST IDEA I'D EVER HEARD" 88

Chapter 9   STARR-ING ANNIE 103

Chapter 10   *ANNIE*: THE MOVIE 109

The Story of Mr. Am 121

Epilogue 145

Index 146

ACKNOWLEDGMENTS

I cannot recall the names of all the hundreds of people who helped me during the year and a half I spent on this project; some of them I never knew. But I thank them all in general, and these in particular: Seymour Barofsky and Esther Margolis of Newmarket Press; Julie Fallowfield of McIntosh & Otis; Bob Reed, Don Michel, Bill Harley, and Arthur Laro of the Tribune Company Syndicate; Dr. Howard Gotlieb and Douglas MacDonald of the Boston University Department of Special Collections; Martin Charnin, Thomas Meehan, Charles Strouse, David Powers, and Barbara Carroll of Broadway's *Annie*; Joe Whitaker and Mary Kay Powell of Rastar; Mary Eger; Leonard Starr, Jud Hurd, Rick Marschall, Harvey Kurtzman, Larry Siegel, Elliott Caplin, Tex Blaisdell, and Stu Reisbord; Lyle Bergmann of Ovaltine; Michele Friedhoffer; William Wills of WGN in Chicago; Chris Steinbrunner; George Longstreth; the New York Public Library; the Greenwich Public Library; Perrot Memorial Library; the Academy of Motion Picture Arts and Sciences; Loren Craft, Jack Sanders, John Hodgson, and Gene Ferrara of the New York *Daily News*. And special thanks from the heart to Alton Slagle, Worth Gatewood, Travis MacTavish, and Katherine Eger.

Bruce Smith
December 1981

FOREWORD

by Worth Gatewood

The life span of all but a handful of comic strips, like that of the mayfly, is short and largely unremarked. Each year, newspaper syndicates search through a flood of presentations from aspiring cartoonists in the faint hope of finding a strip that will fly in the notoriously turbulent skies of the comic strip world. In the main, these offerings range from the preposterous to the merely bad, and the perpetrators are notified with terse politeness that their work is "unsuitable," a word of many definitions, all of them negative.

Occasionally, though, something will come in over the transom that shows signs of life, however feeble. In these few cases the syndicate springs happily into action, somewhat like a pediatrics team dealing with a premature birth. The cartoonist, dazed as if struck by lightning, is called in, his concept is discussed and dissected, his characters are analyzed and often given altered personalities, a story line is agreed upon (and this can be quite different from what the originator had in mind), and the cartoonist is sent on his way, bedazzled by dreams of fame and fortune. The syndicate marshals its marketing troops, an impressive and expensive brochure is prepared, and salesmen are dispatched to beguile editors into publishing what almost surely will become another *Dick Tracy*, a *Blondie*, a *Li'l Abner*. Or perhaps even another *Little Orphan Annie*.

Mr. Gatewood is the former Sunday Editor of the New York *Daily News.*

THE HISTORY OF LITTLE ORPHAN ANNIE

Alas! As an occasionally beguiled former Sunday editor of the New York *Daily News*, traditionally a showcase for the best in comics, I can say that in all but a few instances the promise falls dismally short in reality. A good many strips falter in months, others last a year or so, then expire quietly and with few mourners. The chances of a major success are slim indeed. Over the past ten or twelve years only three strips—Broom-Hilda, Doonesbury and Hagar the Horrible—have caught and held public attention and affection to the degree achieved by the golden oldies of the comics pages. The list of these still-successful strips is long and varied; they offer humor, adventure, fantasy, soap opera, and crime-busting, and each has its hopelessly addicted followers. But this is a fragmented and partisan audience: *Dick Tracy* fans tend to sneer at *Brenda Starr*, *Gasoline Alley* types loathe *Andy Capp*, and so on. Only one strip in the past half-century has managed to attain almost universal appeal, and that one is the subject of Bruce Smith's affectionate and vastly entertaining biohistory: *Little Orphan Annie*.

Annie has long since ceased to be simply a comic-strip figure, a pert, zero-eyed, tousle-haired moppet in a red dress. Like the cowboy of the Old West, she has become part of the American myth, a heroine for all seasons who conquers every adversity and foils every villain with pluck and luck and, of course, a little help from Sandy, Daddy Warbucks, Punjab, and the Asp. And from myth she has become a phenomenom. Left for dead only a few years ago when several cartoonists tried and failed to match the magic of her late creator, Harold Gray, Annie rose from the grave, so to speak, in the hit Broadway musical which at last report had earned $4.3 million in its long run. Actually, Annie wasn't stone-cold dead; a hundred-odd newspapers carried reruns of the thirties' strips with the dialogue edited to excise archaic slang and references that would be incomprehensible to modern readers. And now Annie is the star of a movie musical that promises to be an even bigger hit than the stage version. A truly amazing career for a 57-year-old orphan whose prospects seemed dim at the outset!

As a strip, the old Annie was something of a paradox. She was born in 1924, the peak of what columnist Westbrook Pegler called "the era of wonderful nonsense." It was a time of flaming youth, flappers, bathtub gin, and the Charleston. Comic strips then were just that—comic—and Harold Gray had no more humor in him than his idol, Calvin Coolidge. Who in those frivolous days wanted to read the treacly adventures of a put-upon orphan? Further, Gray's drawing in the early days was primitive, his dialogue was scarcely above the me-Tarzan-you-Jane level, and the plots were as trite as the cowboy

FOREWORD

movies of the time. The conventional wisdom among cartoonists was that Annie would be mercifully fetched to heaven in short order. Only two people had any faith in her: Gray, of course, and Joseph M. Patterson, publisher of the *News*, who had the gift of perceiving gold in comics where others saw only dross.

Their faith was bountifully rewarded. Millions of readers of both sexes and all ages took Annie to their hearts, not knowing that Harold Gray was thumbing his nose at the canons of cartooning. Imbued with a Calvinist morality and a political conservatism slightly to the right of Ivan the Terrible, he injected both into his story line and fiercely rejected criticism from the liberal quarter. In the bleakest days of the Depression, when conservatism as a cause seemed terminally afflicted and most of Gray's readers were staunch supporters of Franklin D. Roosevelt, Annie nonetheless reached the pinnacle of her popularity. Al Capp's enormously popular Li'l Abner did not survive Capp's deepening conservatism in his later years; Annie not only survived but thrived.

But it seemed almost a certainty that she could not survive Gray's death; the magic had apparently died with him. Still, one editor at the *News* was not yet prepared to write her final obituary. "Annie," he said, "is immortal. Don't bet she won't come back in some form or other." And so she did, on Broadway and in Hollywood. Just at a time when millions of Americans, troubled by the turbulence and gnawing uncertainties of recent years, were groping for a return to ideals once thought of as eternal verities, there arose on stage, phoenix-like, the very personification of those ideals—Annie. The tremendous response to the musical led Annie's guardian, the Chicago Tribune–New York News Syndicate, Inc., (since renamed the Tribune Company Syndicate) to launch another search for a cartoonist to put Annie back on the drawing board. The search ended with Leonard Starr, a talented dramatist as well as one of the finest draftsmen in cartooning. Thus Annie was born again in her original form, the comic strip. She's doing splendidly, too.

What is the secret of Annie's broad and lasting appeal? It's very likely that she is what we would all like to be: brave, resolute, shrewd, honest, loyal . . . and a spunky type who takes no guff from anybody. But let Bruce Smith tell you all about her.

Chapter 1

ONLY AN ORPHAN

The oldest little girl in the world was born in 1924. Little Orphan Annie has been living the hard-knocks life since then, and in all that time she hasn't aged a day. She's still 11 years old.

In all that time, too, she hasn't lost her appeal. She's one of only a handful of comic-strip characters who have managed to retain their popularity over the decades. And not just on paper: three generations, so far, have followed her exploits in the funny papers, on the radio, on Broadway, and at the movies.

Annie appeals, as the old saying goes, to "children of all ages." When the *Little Orphan Annie* comic strip was first begun, it was aimed at adults, not children. The theory was that children didn't read newspapers. The theory was wrong.

The strip was unique in that it could be read on more than one level. Just as a Marx Brothers movie can be appreciated either for its slapstick comedy or for its biting satire, *Little Orphan Annie* could be read for the charm of a little girl wandering through the world, or for the political tract it frequently became.

As Charles Dickens had done a century earlier, Annie's creator, Harold Gray, wrote morality stories. And like Dickens', they appeared in serial form.

In a sense, Gray was also an historian. He took his story ideas for *Little Orphan Annie* from the headlines on the front page. The strip became a chronicle of its time, reflecting the changing mood of the country as it went from the prosperity of the Twenties to the poverty of the Thirties, from a war of bullets and bombs in the Forties to the wars of words and ideas in the Fifties and Sixties. The long gestation of the Broadway show *Annie* continued the chronicle tradition, although inadvertently. Originally written as an antidote to the pessimism and despair of the Watergate era, the show finally opened at about the same time a new president, Jimmy Carter, took office and promised to give America "a government as good as its people."

Gray was a political archconservative, armed with a short fuse and a long reach into millions of American households. His war against Franklin D. Roosevelt's New Deal during the Depression stirred intense debate across the country. It made him many enemies, but he never backed down.

Much of that political content was dropped from the strip after Gray died, and is almost entirely missing from the Broadway show and film based on Gray's characters. Nonetheless, Annie is more popular now than she's ever been. The explanation for that lies in the characters themselves and the traits Gray assigned to them.

Annie belongs in the same league with such other fictional characters as Huckleberry Finn, Robin Hood, and Alice in Wonderland. Her story will never grow old with passing time or wearisome in repetition, because like them, she is a character, not just a caricature.

She's a little girl who doesn't think or act like one; she's a child with the mind of an adult.

She hasn't been to school much and her way of speaking is a little rough around the edges, but she's very smart, and savvy in the ways of the world.

She's tough, but only when she has to be. She's got a big heart, and a soft spot for the few people she meets who are even more unfortunate than she is.

She's an underdog, an outcast, without family or background. Her past is as blank as her empty eyes.

She's powerless. She can't fly, or see through brick walls, or lift freight trains with one hand. She has to work her way out of jams the same way the rest of us do.

She's incorruptible, sustained only by her own goodness in the evil places she travels to.

Her motto is short and sweet: "Tell the truth, work hard, save your money, and keep your nose tidy." As her creator, Harold Gray, once remarked, "That's good advice for any kid, and especially for an orphan."

Although she's an orphan, Annie is by no means alone in the world. She has her faithful dog, Sandy, and her adopted "Daddy,"

ONLY AN ORPHAN

Oliver Warbucks, who happens to be the richest man in the world. Life could be cushy with him around, except he's never given her so much as a dime and is always going away on long, mysterious business trips, leaving Annie and Sandy alone to stumble innocently into the most bloodcurdling adventures.

Over the years they've had to tangle with a rogues' gallery of crooks and gangsters, foreign spies, corrupt politicians, murderers, pinkos, misfits, enemies of democracy, and every agent of villainy imaginable. They always manage to come out okay in the end—and to plunge almost immediately into another predicament.

Harold Gray had two rules he made Annie live by: she could never reach a "happy ending," and she could never grow up. None of the surrogate fathers and mothers who have guided her destiny since his death have seen fit to overrule him. In fact, they've changed remarkably little. From that fateful day back in 1924 when she heaved a bowl of mush in mean Miss Asthma's face and shouted "Leapin' Lizards!" for the first time, Annie has remained just what Gray intended for her to be: "Tougher than hell, with a heart of gold and a fast left."

She's good, all right. But she's no goody-goody. She always plays by the rule book, but once in a while forgets the part that says it isn't ladylike to belt a bully in the chops. Annie has a license to use both ends of that old slogan, "Might makes right."

Her Daddy Warbucks, on the other hand, has never read a copy of anyone's rule book. He writes his own as he goes along. From time to time, his way of getting things done doesn't quite square with civilized behavior, but when you're the richest man in the world you can't afford to let yourself get bogged down in technicalities. If Warbucks has ever regretted his ruthless methods, he has yet to show it.

Only the youngest of Annie's followers fail to recognize the symbolism in her unique relationship with Daddy Warbucks. If Freud were still around, he'd have a field day with it; as it is, plenty of his disciples have taken a crack at it.

The bond between Annie and Daddy boils down to the mutual devotion of opposites: a man whose wealth and power isolate him from the warmth of human touch, and a poor, weak child, alone in the world.

Nobody knows where Annie got her name, any more than where she came from. It's possible—but by no means certain—that a poem called "Little Orphant Annie" had a lot to do with Annie's origin. The poem was written in 1885 by James Whitcomb Riley, famous throughout the Midwest as the "Hoosier Poet."

Riley's verses were folksy, homespun tales that reflected everyday life in the farming communities and small towns of his native Indiana. In this particular poem, he was expanding on a character named Little Orphant Annie, whom he had used in an earlier poem and who was said to be modeled on a real orphan girl employed in the Riley household. In those days, before the advent of social-welfare agencies, a child who lost its parents was completely dependent on the mercy of relatives or neighbors. When an orphan moved into another home, he or she was usually treated more as a hired hand than a new member of the family.

"Little Orphant Annie" became one of Riley's most popular poems through his public readings of it. Small children were particularly fond of it for the powerful, thumping refrain:

> Little Orphant Annie's come to our house to stay,
> An' wash the cups an' saucers up, an' bresh the crumbs away,
> An' shoo the chickens off the porch, an' dust the hearth, an'
>   sweep,
> An' make the fire, an' bake the bread, an' earn her board-an'-
>   keep;
> An' all us other childern, when the supper-things is done,
> We set around the kitchen fire an' has the mostest fun
> A'list'nin' to the witch-tales 'at Annie tells about
>   An' the Gobble'uns 'at gits you
>   Ef you
>   Don't
>   Watch
>   Out!

The poem reached a wide audience in the Midwest, and was surely known around Kankakee, Illinois, where Gray was born on January 20, 1894.

Was Riley's poem the source of Annie's name, and perhaps her colorful way of speaking? It's a question Gray never answered, and it's far too late to ask him now.

The moment of Annie's creation evokes a sentimental image. One imagines Gray, the struggling young artist, sitting at his drawing board late one night, the floor around him littered with crumpled, rejected sketches of the comic-strip character he wanted so desperately to draw.

Suddenly, his head perks up as the pen beneath his fingers works some idle scratchings on the paper into the outline of a small figure. As his pen fills in more lines, a little girl takes shape. She has short,

ONLY AN ORPHAN

curly hair, an upturned nose, and big, round eyes—the pupils can be filled in later. Finally, red-eyed and exhausted but delighted with his creation, the artist leans back and studies the figure he's created, a triumphant smile on his face.

Pushing sentiment brusquely aside, the reality was not so. Harold Gray did not set out to create *Little Orphan Annie* any more than Christopher Columbus set sail to discover America. They shared the same dream—finding a way to vast wealth—but neither of them knew where he was going until he got there.

Annie wasn't the first cartoon character Gray had come up with, and she wouldn't have been the last if someone hadn't agreed to take a chance on her. He wanted to do a comic strip, and if Annie couldn't have given him the opportunity, he would have chucked her in the wastebasket with all his other failed ideas without a backward glance.

As it happened, Annie caught on. So she stayed. Later on, Daddy and Sandy caught on, too. If they hadn't, Gray would have given them the same heave-ho he gave the two Mrs. Warbucks and other characters he created for the strip who didn't cut the mustard.

In short, the birth of Annie did not take place in a single act of inspired genius. It was, however, a very clever one, and the most admirable thing about Gray's creation is the fact that Annie could never be changed. Even when she passed beyond his reach and other hands guided her along, she remained the "simple orphan kid" he always wanted her to be. As a result, Annie is as close to taking a real breath of air as any imaginary being has ever been.

Chapter 2

"THE KID LOOKS LIKE A PANSY TO ME"

Annie's tough because her life is tough, and that began at the beginning. She was a notion that just barely made it onto paper and ink. Nobody—including the man who brought her to life—expected her to survive for long. She fooled him, along with every other skeptic, and became the most successful female in American newspaper history. Looking back now, it's easy to see that she was in the right place at the right time. But it didn't seem like it then.

The time was 1924. There were 100 million-plus citizens of the United States, including, for the first time, American Indians. Calvin Coolidge was President. Booze was illegal, but women had been voting for four years, and that year witnessed the election of females as governors of Texas and Wyoming. George Gershwin wrote *Rhapsody in Blue*. The movies were still silent, radio was an infant, and television was decades in the future. The printed word was supreme, and the mass medium was newspapers.

The place was the New York *News*. A fledgling tabloid in existence only five years, the newspaper was trying to make more secure the foothold it had in a fiercely competitive market. At least a dozen other papers were clawing and scratching for the same set of readers. It was a no-holds-barred fracas in which circulation was the name of the game and anything that could get and hold readers was a valuable commodity. Among the most valuable were comic strips, the "funny papers." Editors everywhere, and particularly in New York, were constantly on the lookout for ideas for new comic strips, most of all "story" strips that featured a standing cast of characters and a plot line that continued from one day to the next. Those built circulation.

Among the most vigilant—and successful—of the editors was Joseph Medill Patterson of the New York *News*, the paper he had founded with his cousin Robert McCormack, publisher of the Chicago *Tribune.* "Captain" Patterson and "Colonel" McCormack had conceived the *News* during a chat in a French farmyard during World War I, when they were both serving in the U.S. Army (their respective titles of rank remained with both men for the rest of their lives). The two newspapering cousins had seen and admired Lord Northcliffe's London *Illustrated News,* a highly successful venture in the tabloid format—only half the size of a conventional "broadsheet" newspaper—which ran to big pictures and spicier news content than most of its more staid, gray rivals on Fleet Street. Patterson and McCormack agreed to launch a similar paper in New York after the war, and they did.

For its first few years, the *News* was a satellite operation. Patterson directed its staff from Chicago, where he and McCormack co-edited the *Tribune.* By 1924, the *News* was on solid ground; New York's straphangers had accepted the paper's small, convenient format and its lively content. But competitors had responded with imitations. What the *News* needed was more readers, and Patterson was out to get them any way he could.

The Captain had a keen instinct for features, and a special knack for the comics. Many of the strips that were running in the *News* had been his ideas. In 1917, he'd conceived *The Gumps,* a story strip depicting middle-class life that became enormously popular and made a wealthy man of Sidney Smith, the artist who drew it. The following year, Patterson tapped the automotive craze with *Gasoline Alley.* In 1921, Gotham's working girls found their reflections in *Winnie Winkle,* and two years later a lovable lout named *Moon Mullins* showed up on the same pages. All were successful, but Patterson, as usual, wanted more. He advertised far and wide his receptivity to any and all suggestions for new comic strips.

The most persistent—and least successful—of those suggestors was a former *Tribune* staff artist named Harold Gray.

An Indiana farmboy, Gray had developed a talent for drawing at an early age. He landed his first professional job at the Lafayette *Morning Journal* by selling the publisher on the idea of political cartoons at a dollar apiece. He spent a summer at the *Journal,* not only drawing cartoons but soliciting advertising, collecting bills, and bringing in news stories.

Gray had his sights set on a writing career, and hoped to study journalism at either the University of Wisconsin or the University of Missouri. But money was scarce, so he enrolled at the hometown school, Purdue University. Even then, he had to take a year off midway through to earn money for tuition, and he dug ditches 10 hours a day for 20 cents an hour. When he returned to Purdue, he became art editor of the yearbook, the *Debris*, and between classes, he liked to relax with a few rounds of boxing.

The morning after he graduated from Purdue in 1917, Gray was on the milk train to Chicago, with $13 in his pocket and dreams of becoming a successful artist in his head. To stretch his money, he got off the train in Hammond, Indiana, and rode the streetcar into Chicago. His destination was the Tribune Tower and the office of John T. McCutcheon, at the time the dean of Midwestern cartoonists, and a Purdue alumnus. McCutcheon introduced Gray to the paper's art editor, who didn't have an opening just then, but Gray managed to get himself on the payroll as a cub reporter, at $15 a week. Within a short time, he was transferred to the art department.

He left the paper briefly to serve as a bayonet instructor in the army, and when he came back he piled up so much freelance business on the side that he was able to establish his own commercial art studio on North Dearborn Street. In 1920, he quit the *Tribune* staff because he was making four times his salary freelancing. That same year, he landed the plum job of assistant to Sidney Smith, who drew *The Gumps*.

Then as now, a popular comic strip, distributed widely by one of the newspaper syndicates, could make its author a very large sum of money. That was certainly the case with Smith, who was the highest-paid comic-strip artist of his time. Bitten by the creative bug and encouraged by Smith, Gray was determined to draw a comic strip of his own.

"Comic brainstorms attacked me with increasing frequency and violence as 1924 approached," he recalled in an article he wrote some 30 years later. "But the Captain always seemed able to reduce any swelling of the ego and to suppress my many abortive lunges for fame and fortune." To put it more bluntly, Patterson shot down every trial balloon that Gray sent up.

Gray didn't give up, though. He kept sketching characters and showing them to Sid Smith, who would offer his opinion and suggestions for each. One of the sketches was of a small child, whom Gray told Smith would be an orphan boy.

"Simplicity was essential," he remembered. "An orphan starts with no relatives or friends, or any other complications. Sid said the child must be clean and cute and sweet, to appeal to women readers. So the kid was clean and had golden curls."

Gray titled the strip "Little Orphan Ottor," worked up a dozen sketches of the boy in various poses, and showed them to Patterson. He was braced for the familiar slap of rejection. Instead, the editor was bemused. And for reasons known then and now only to himself, Patterson decided to give Gray's orphan a break. But with one important alteration: "The kid looks like a pansy to me," the Captain said with a scowl. "Put a skirt on him and we'll call it 'Little Orphan Annie.'"

There is a second version of Annie's birth, a much less colorful account given by Gray to *Editor & Publisher* magazine in 1951. He told of his early days as a cub reporter for the *Tribune* and how he used to roam the streets of Chicago on the prowl for stories. "One early morning on the streets," the *E & P* article stated, "he caught sight of a little gamine, quite evidently in the so-called age of innocence, wise as an old owl. 'I talked to this little kid, and liked her right away,'" Gray was quoted as saying. "'She had common sense, knew how to take care of herself. She had to. Her name was Annie. At the time, some 40 strips were using boys as the main characters; only three were using girls. I chose Annie for mine, and made her an orphan, so she'd have no family, no tangling alliances, but freedom to go where she pleased.'"

Given Gray's disposition, and his gift for inspired storytelling, the first version seems far more believable than the second. In the many articles he wrote over the years explaining how Annie was created, Gray always gave the first version as the "official" account, and always gave Patterson plenty of credit for helping to bring Annie into the world. Perhaps, like many other people who are asked the same question over and over again, Gray decided to amuse himself at *E & P*'s expense by fabricating a new answer. Maybe it was even the truth. There's no way of knowing for sure now.

Little Orphan Annie made its first appearance on page 26 of the *News* on Monday, August 5, 1924, a few pages back from the editorials, which were always headed by the paper's "Platform For New York: 1—A Seat for Every Child in the Public Schools. 2—A 5-Cent Fare and Better Service. 3—Improved Traffic Conditions on the Street. 4—A Bridge Across the Hudson to New Jersey. 5—Stricter Regulation of the Sale of Pistols. 6—More Parks for the People."

Gray and Patterson had worked together to plot the first few strips, during which the Captain laid down another dictum: "Make it for grown-ups. Kids don't buy papers, their parents do."

On that Monday morning, readers of the *Daily News* were confronted with a slip of a girl with hair so frizzy it seemed she'd stuck her finger in an electrical socket, empty-saucer eyes, and a drab dress with many patches sewn on it.

There was no formal introduction. She just showed up. From the start, *Little Orphan Annie* bore a headline every day, and on that first day it read: "Wants To Leave Her Home." The opening panel showed a tall, bespectacled, prune-faced woman shaking her finger at a little girl who stood with her hands clasped behind her back.

"Now Annie," the woman said, "if these people who are coming to the 'home' tomorrow should adopt you I hope you'll always remember what a lot we've done for you here. You have been sheltered, clothed and fed since you were a baby entirely by charity. You should be grateful."

"Yessum, Miss Asthma," the little girl replied, without the slightest indication of gratitude.

The next panel showed Annie on her hands and knees, scrubbing the floor and muttering to herself, "When she keeps reminding me I'm an orphan and that I'm a charity girl it makes me *hate* her and *hate* the 'home' and I *hate* myself, too, for being so poor. Gee, I wish some nice folks would adopt me. Then I could have a real papa and mama like other kids."

The soliloquy continued in the third panel, where Annie was washing dishes: "And then maybe I could have two dresses and there wouldn't always be dishes to wash and scrubbing and mending. But I wouldn't mind working hard every minute if only they weren't always telling me I'm an orphan."

In the last panel, Annie was kneeling down saying her bedtime prayers: "And please make me a real good little girl so some nice people will adopt me. Then I can have a papa and mama to love. And if it's not too much trouble I'd like a dolly, too. Amen."

After that opening-day tearjerker, Gray settled down to flesh out his characters. The next day, a seemingly nice couple with a small son showed up at the "home." But when the boy made fun of Annie's tattered dress, she walloped him in the kisser. They left in a huff, with the mother saying over her shoulder, "If I had a rowdy like that, I'd certainly train her." Annie came right back at her with, "Aw, train your own brat!"

That little scene put Annie in big dutch with Miss Asthma and got her assigned to extra work. A few days later, while sweeping up in front of the orphanage office, she overheard Miss Asthma telling a visitor about how she came to be placed in the orphanage—something that Annie herself didn't know.

"Let's see, it's in this file here," Miss Asthma began. "Annie herself may have these records when she is 21 if she desires, but not until

10

then. Now I will read all we have concerning her. There are several pages and it is quite interesting, I might say. Her *parents* . . ."

But at that point, she got up and shut the door, leaving Annie—and readers—to muse about her past: "Well I'll be a *sardine*! What do you know about that? So I have a history with parents in it and everything. I'm glad I have *something* of my own, even a history—and parents. I never could be sure whether orphans ever had any parents. I can't remember any. Wait till I'm 21. I'll have to hurry and grow up real soon. Isn't it funny to be someone but not know who?"

Life in the orphanage invented by Gray was every bit as grim as its real-life counterparts. The food was bad, the beds were lumpy, the clothes were raggedy, and Miss Asthma's rotten disposition shrouded the place in perpetual gloom. Gray established Annie as, basically, a good kid struggling through a bad situation with as much cheerfulness as could be expected.

Midway through the second week, Annie was told by Miss Asthma that a Mrs. Warbucks would be coming the next day and might decide to adopt her. A big, buxom woman, this Mrs. Warbucks arrived in a chauffeured limousine, wearing the trappings of a dedicated social climber. She explained in a very condescending manner that it was the *duty* of wealthy individuals to take someone less fortunate under their wing, and she agreed to take Annie home with her—but only on trial.

They were driven to the Warbucks mansion, staffed by servants and decorated with paintings and sculpture. Annie was quick to make herself at home, but her rambunctious nature and colorful language soon put her on the wrong side of Mrs. Warbucks, who was revealed as a phony wanting only to impress her society friends with her charity. Annie, cleaned up and well dressed, was expected to be polite and silent, like the servants, the paintings and the sculpture.

But if it was well-behaved window dressing that Mrs. Warbucks was after, she had picked out the wrong orphan. Annie's natural curiosity, energy, and direct way of speaking brought the lady of the house no end of distress. Among other things, she slid down the bannisters, knocked over a couple of priceless vases, offended the houseguests, and punched the obnoxious neighbor boy.

In the midst of all that turmoil, some six weeks after Annie's first appearance, Gray made a move that was to insure his fortune, although he had no idea of that at the time. He introduced a new character by the name of Oliver Warbucks. His wife explained to Annie that he was away on one of his frequent business trips, and for several days the entire household bustled to prepare for the arrival of "the master."

11

Warbucks burst through the front door like a longshoreman. A bald-headed, tough-talking fellow, he was "new money" in the flesh. He slapped the servants on the back, playfully insulted his wife, stepped on the dog, and didn't even notice Annie at first. He finally caught sight of her on September 27, 1924; it was a memorable moment in comic-strip history.

"Say, whose kid are you?" he demanded to know.

"I'm nobody's kid, Mr. Warbucks," Annie replied meekly, "I'm just an orphan Mrs. Warbucks took on trial."

"WHAT? On trial, eh? Listen here, don't you ever dare to call me *Mr. Warbucks* again!"

"YES SIR!" she replied, drawing back in fear.

Suddenly, he reached down and scooped her up into his arms. "You call me DADDY—*see?*"

It was a delightful scene, and a daring one. Gray was going against the grain by depicting a rich man sympathetically. In most other comic strips at that time, the wealthy were shown as either greedy opportunists or bumbling nincompoops. That a big shot might take a shine to a poor little stranger was a peculiar notion. Even more peculiar was the name Gray gave him.

"If I'd had any idea he'd be a regular character, I'd have never given him that name," the cartoonist said years later. But Warbucks got his handle the same way many of the characters in *Little Orphan Annie* got theirs over the years. Gray used a system that was similar in some ways to Dickens'—a person was named for what he did in life. Among the hundreds of people he named that way were Doc Scalpel, Judge Tort, Iziah D. Posit the banker, William Tell the reporter, Fred Fritter the town bum, Old Tom Trowel the gardener, Herb Root the druggist, and Al Apathy the "typical citizen."

Warbucks was a munitions manufacturer who'd made huge profits during World War I. That hardly made him a sympathetic figure, but he was not, Gray contended, the dastardly villain he was made out to be in subsequent years. "Sure, he made his money in the war, but not in profiteering. He represented the rough-hewn industrialist, the pirate of international finance. I patterned Warbucks after Big Business in the thought that Big Business was being maligned."

When Warbucks first held her in his arms, though, Annie didn't care what he did for a living or what he might have been a symbol of. All she cared about was that he was the first person who had shown her any kindness and affection in a long, long time. As they got acquainted over the next few days, she learned that he was a self-made man who had owned a small machine shop when the war broke out. Could he help it if the government gave him huge defense contracts that made him rich? Clearly, here was a man with deeply hurt feelings who believed nobody liked him because he'd made money from the war.

There they were—the orphan nobody wanted and the munitions maker nobody liked. Not quite, though. He obviously wanted her to stick around, and she just as obviously had taken a liking to him. It was the skin and bones of one of the most beautiful friendships in modern fiction. It would take Gray several years to flesh out these two characters and fully exploit their dramatic potential, but less than two months after he'd started *Little Orphan Annie*, he had hit on the rich formula that would guarantee its success.

From then on, Annie and Daddy—and Harold Gray—had it made. The strip had survived its first crucial weeks (something that five other new strips that started on the same day had not). Patterson, cautious in his enthusiasm for *Little Orphan Annie*, had allowed it to run only in the *News'* limited-circulation "pink edition" at first, and only on weekdays. By early November he was confident enough to order the strip into all editions of both the *News* and the Chicago *Tribune*, and he asked Gray to begin drawing a full-page weekly episode for the Sunday color comics sections. Patterson also made the new strip available to papers all over the country through the Chicago Tribune–New York News Syndicate (since renamed the Tribune Company Syndicate).

Nobody, not even Gray, could have known then how popular *Little Orphan Annie* was destined to become. He continued to work as Sidney Smith's assistant on *The Gumps* while drawing *Annie*. But he began to think something big might be up.

"I felt as much as any dub might feel who has been groping and stumbling around in the dark and suddenly discovers himself high in the air on a tight wire," he recalled in 1951. "I had to go forward. Certain characteristics of the strip seemed to be popular. The only sane course was to stick to that straight line, and avoid fancy steps, at least till I got my balance. I made my full share of blunders, and still do, but I never strayed beyond grabbing distance of that tight wire, that central theme of the strip, that Annie is just a simple orphan kid after all."

Still later, Gray shed some more light on those crucial first few weeks: "I could never bring myself to draw Annie as an innocent, sheltered, prissy little angel, or as a smart-aleck little snit that everyone would love to skewer on a hot poker. She must be an orphan of the toughest city streets and alleys; her school, the world as she met it; her teachers, the people around her—the good and the bad, the brave and the cowards, and especially the ones like most of us who

THE HISTORY OF LITTLE ORPHAN ANNIE

are pretty much a mixture of all the sins and virtues. A level-eyed, straight-backed, courageous little child usually brings out the best in even the worst of us."

After three decades of drawing Annie, he thought he knew her pretty well and why the public had latched onto her so quickly: "She was not a 'comic.' She didn't attempt to panic the public every day or send millions into hysterics with her game of wit. Life to her was deadly serious. She had to be hard to survive and she meant to survive. Life to hundreds of thousands of New York *News* readers was also deadly serious. They, too, had to be hard, and they meant to survive. Perhaps Annie unwittingly at first touched a common chord. Anyway, she made it. She caught the fancy of the taxi drivers, night waitresses, the late Broadway crowds, the mass of other folks also trying desperately to 'make it.' "

It angered Gray no end that some people thought he got the idea for Annie and Daddy Warbucks from one of the most celebrated sex scandals of the Twenties. The allegation, though false, was widely believed; in his book, *Thy Neighbor's Wife*, Gay Talese repeated it.

Any relationship between a rich tycoon and a poor, beguiling girl naturally bears some interest. None in modern American history could match the scintillating story of Edward West Browning and Frances Heenan, known to the readers of virtually every newspaper in the country in 1926 as "Daddy and Peaches."

Browning was the scion of a wealthy, respectable New York City family. He had joined his father in the real estate business at an early age and kept his nose to the grindstone night and day until he had amassed a fortune estimated at $30 million. Such a diligent business-man was he that the allure of the opposite sex went unnoticed until he reached middle age.

At 40, he was smitten by a pretty blond clerk named Nellie. They were married, and after several years of childless marriage, the Brownings adopted two small girls. In 1923, however, Nellie ran off to Paris with a dentist from the Bronx and the couple was divorced, with Browning retaining custody of the youngest girl, nine-year-old Dorothy.

A bachelor again at 47, Browning took to attending teenage social affairs. "I've worked my head off all my life," he told his shocked business colleagues. "Now, I'm having a little amusement."

At one such soirée, a high school sorority dance at the McAlpin Hotel on Broadway in March 1926, Browning set eyes on 15-year-old Frances Heenan, the daughter of a divorced nurse. Subse-quent newspaper accounts described the girl as "well-built in a full-blown way, particularly in the legs." She had blond hair, a pretty face, and what Browning told reporters was "the bloom of youth."

He was infatuated. Three days after they met, he announced that he was in love with her. The press dubbed them "Daddy and Peaches," and photographers accompanied him on his courting calls to the Heenans' fifth-floor walk-up apartment.

Daddy proposed. Peaches accepted. Mrs. Heenan approved. But the Children's Society did not, and filed charges for improper guardianship against Mrs. Heenan. The police, the board of education, and the clergy all took an interest. The New York State Legislature debated enactment of more stringent laws concerning child marriages.

They were all too late. Daddy and Peaches had a quickie wedding in a small upstate town. The groom was 36 years older than the bride, who was described in the local paper as "plump and pouty." The happy couple returned to New York City and conducted a very public honeymoon highlighted by the child bride's spending sprees in the city's most exclusive stores. "Peaches is spending $1,000 a day," Daddy gloated. "And it makes me love my little girl all the more!"

His ecstasy was short-lived. Less than six months after they tied the knot, Peaches walked out. Daddy was devastated. During the ensuing court trial, the public drank up the lurid details of nights in the Browning boudoir like mosquitoes at a Fourth of July picnic. Peaches told all: midnight romps in the nude, his insistence that they eat their breakfast in bed with no clothes on, vivid descriptions of his unusual preferences. Worst of all, she accused him of corrupting the morals of his young adopted daughter, Dorothy.

At the end of the sordid proceedings, Browning got the separation he had sought and Peaches lost the $300-a-week alimony he had been paying her. But in a bizarre development, his request for a divorce was denied, leaving Daddy and Peaches husband and wife. She went into show business, performing in nightclubs and burlesque houses, capitalizing on all the free publicity. He sold off many of his real estate holdings to establish a charitable trust fund and took to prowling the dance halls along Broadway, always accompanied by a male chaperone. They were still legally married when he died of a cerebral hemorrhage in 1934, and his will granted Peaches $170,000 in cash and property, which sustained her until her own death in 1956.

Those who see the prototypes for *Little Orphan Annie* in Daddy Browning and Peaches are using faulty chronology. Annie and Daddy Warbucks were the best of friends in the funny papers by the time Peaches and Daddy Browning made the front page. And even if they hadn't been, Gray's stern Midwestern morality wouldn't have permitted him to entertain the notion of turning such rancid goings-on into the vehicle for his life's work. If anything, Daddy Browning and Peaches were eerie examples of life imitating—and, in this case, perverting—art.

Having forged a bond of mutual trust and affection between his two leading characters, Gray dispatched Daddy Warbucks on one of his famous "business trips," leaving Annie in the lurch for the first of what would be umpteen times over the years. No sooner was he out the door on his way to Siberia than Mrs. Warbucks packed Annie back to Miss Asthma's, where she was subsequently adopted by a slavedriver named Mrs. Bottle, who took her home to "Pop" Bottle and their children, the "seven half-pints." Life with the Bottles wasn't much more pleasant than it had been at the orphanage, but in January 1925, Gray gave her a companion—a frisky brown puppy she promptly named Sandy. He was all ears, nose, and tail then, and has the distinction now of being the only one of Harold Gray's major characters ever to age naturally: he grew to adulthood and stayed there.

Annie and Sandy went on the lam, and eventually ended up on a farm owned by poor but kindly Mr. and Mrs. Silo. After a few months of bucolic adventures, Daddy Warbucks located her and took her and Sandy home with him, over the strenuous objections of Mrs. Warbucks.

That began a sequence that lasted through the fall of 1925 and demonstrated vividly to Patterson and Gray that the year-old strip had become as much a fixture of American breakfast tables as cream in the pitcher and jam on the toast.

Installed once again at the Warbucks mansion, Annie and Daddy—and Sandy, too—await the impending return from Europe of the old battle-axe.

"I shouldn't admit it, Annie, but I sort of dread to see the Mrs. come home. It's not like it used to be," Daddy confided. "I can remember when we were first hooked. We had a little three-room flat. I was foreman in the rollin' mill. We both worked hard and we thought we were poor. But we had happiness. Then I began to make dough. Money, money, money. I wanted to make her happy, see? But it was all a mistake, I guess. We're not happy any more. Instead of happiness, we've got just a wad of dough."

Touched by his candor, Annie put her arms around his neck and comforted him. "Don't you worry, Daddy," she said. "Everything will be jake someday."

Someday, maybe, but not in the short term. Mrs. Warbucks arrived home and not only did she throw a fit when she found Annie there, but announced that she had in tow an oily young man named Selbert Adlebert Piffleberry, of noble European ancestry, who would be staying indefinitely. Annie quickly spotted young Selbert (whom she addressed by all his initials: "Sap") for a phony, and when his uncle, the equally greasy Count De Tour, arrived, Daddy soon sized him up as a four-flusher, too. The count, Warbucks learned through his mysterious intelligence network, was a shady character with a violent past. It seemed that his wife's desperate attempts to be accepted by "society" had brought into Warbucks' own home a pair of vipers intent on nothing short of the ruination of his South American businesses. Day after day, their slimy plans unfolded.

Patterson watched the story progress with growing concern. Gray seemed to be taking Little Orphan Annie away from the course the Captain had originally set. He was disturbed that she had left the wholesome life on the Silos' farm for the Warbucks mansion with its silver place settings, servants, limousines. Then came the machinations of international high finance and foreign intrigue. The last straw came when Mrs. Warbucks secretly ordered the servants to take Sandy out and shoot him. It was no good, Patterson decided. Annie was putting on the Ritz. What was this poor little orphan girl doing living in a mansion, surrounded by European nobility? He ordered the strip out of the Chicago Tribune.

When the morning edition of the Tribune hit the streets on October 27, 1925—without Little Orphan Annie—the reaction from readers was immediate. The Tribune's telephone switchboard lit up like a Christmas tree. "Where's Annie?" was the relentless question. Copy boys, reporters, even editors scrambled to meet the tidal wave of protest. A bomb threat was received.

Patterson was stunned. The next morning, the Tribune printed two Little Orphan Annie strips, and a front-page apology that promised that never again would Annie be left out of the paper. But Patterson wanted to know what exactly there was about Gray's strip that could command such a powerful following. So he asked his readers a question: "Should Annie and her dog, Sandy, be permitted to remain at the home of her latest foster-father, the wealthy and kind-hearted Mr. Warbucks, or should she be returned to the humble but pleasant home of her farmer friends, Mr. and Mrs. Silo?"

So many letters were received that they filled the Tribune's "Letters to the Editor" columns completely for two days. One of them, written by a woman named Minnie McIntyre Wallace of Beloit, Wisconsin, remains to this day one of the most eloquent descriptions of Annie's universal appeal:

Dear Mr. Gray, You have achieved rainbow's end when your creation, Orphan Annie, was made the subject of a column of front page stuff. It is always pleasant to know that merit is recognized. Annie is certainly popular and I want to give you my version of why she has made such a hit.

First—because she is the voice of the people; second, because she is democratic in the true sense of the word, warm of heart, sympathetic, strong for the underdog; third, because she is not dazzled by wealth or shoddy gentility; fourth, because she is the eternal child that lives in the hearts of men and women; fifth, because one never knows down what lane she will run next; sixth, because she loves animals and nature, bees and buds and berries and bossy cows. Children love her—adults sigh for their own lost spontaneity and initiative of youth, seeing them in her.

Don't let anyone tell you how to run Annie's life. You are the master of her fate and the joy of her is the whimsical surprise of her adventures. She would always be the same wherever she lived.

I am afraid you have saddled yourself with an old man of the sea in Annie. She is immortal, for she is the ingenious, plucky, resolute, honest, courageous spirit of young America. We are with her in everything she does.

Other letters were less analytical and more directly to the point. "Send her and Sandy to Mr. and Mrs. Silo quick," wrote a woman from London Mills, Illinois. "The atmosphere of the home she is in now is not for a dog, to say nothing of a little girl. She still can be Daddy Warbucks' girl and have the mother's love and care that Mrs. Silo will give her. But whatever you do, don't leave her out entirely again. She's the best part of the paper."

From Auburn, Indiana, came a letter that read: "Little Orphan Annie is the only kiddie in our family of two adults, and yesterday she was away and joy was the most disappearing thing we had in our home. Don't do it again."

A railroad clerk in Chicago wrote, "Was very much relieved and probably saved from committing crime when Orphan Annie reappeared today. I should never again have bought another *Trib* if you had left Annie out."

A Chicago housewife said her breakfast coffee "failed to have its usual aroma" after she discovered Annie missing from the paper. And the foothills of what would become a mountain of mail over the years concerned with Sandy's well-being assured Gray that Sandy was "one-half the interest for dog-lovers."

Patterson, soundly rebuked but solidly convinced that the kid who "looked like a pansy" was America's favorite comic-strip heroine, never again doubted Gray's judgment or censored his story lines. The cartoonist was given *carte blanche*.

Gray cheerfully resumed the dark tale of foreign intrigue in the Warbucks household, bringing Daddy home in time to save Sandy and churning up more of Count De Tour's sinister activities. Incredibly, Mrs. Warbucks remained blind to the evil doings being hatched right before her eyes. She gave Daddy an ultimatum: either Annie left, or she would.

"Listen, Daddy, it's all right," Annie said to him. "Send me away some place so Mrs. Warbucks will be happy again. I don't want to make trouble for anybody."

Daddy refused to even consider it, so Annie decided to take matters into her own hands.

"Well, Sandy," she said as she packed her things, "we gotta do it. There isn't any way out 'tall. He'll feel bad 'bout our leavin', I know, but 'twon't be anything like if *she* left . . . We'll get along most anywhere. We're both orphans and don't count anyway, I guess. Maybe someday we'll find a home where somebody doesn't hate us."

The next morning, when Daddy found the note Annie left for him, he turned on his wife with the fury of a full-force gale. "*You* drove her out," he screamed. "A poor, sweet little kid who was just trying to be friends—a little youngster who never had a decent break in her life. And *you* made it so nasty for her she's *gone*. You and yer four-flushing, third-rate society pals!"

With that he pulled on his coat, jammed his hat on his head, and went for the door. Count De Tour made the mistake of being in front of him, so Daddy picked him up and booted him in the rear end into the umbrella stand, slammed the door behind him, and went out to look for Annie.

So began the one-man search party that over the years rivaled Telemachus' quest for Ulysses. For decades afterward, Annie and Daddy would be periodically separated, only to be reunited at some crucial moment in the plot.

Thanksgiving Day 1925 found Daddy, Annie, and Sandy sitting happily around the table in the home of the Silos. But there was sorrow in the household of Harold Gray in suburban Lombard, Illinois. His young wife, Doris, had died at home on November 22 after a long illness. She was only 28; they had been married four years.

Her husband's mourning was tempered by the work load he bore from his comic strip's success. *Little Orphan Annie* had become a full-time occupation, and Gray seemed to revel in it. He was not a gregarious man, but clippings from the *Tribune* indicate that he was out and about a good deal during the late Twenties. In the summer of 1926, he and Annie were guests of honor at Chicago's annual orphans' picnic, where he entertained some 4,200 homeless children with his sketchings of Annie and Sandy. He took to the drawing board publicly again the following year at an exhibit of Indiana artists' work in the Marshall Field galleries. He was a subject of a filmed interview by Pathé Review in 1928.

Four years after Doris died, Gray remarried. His bride was Winifred Frost, who worked at the local movie house. A small, attractive, cheerful woman, she would be his bookkeeper, researcher, confidante, and partner in "Gray & Gray," the business they founded together, and would outlive him by a year. After a honeymoon trip to the East Coast, they returned to Lombard. They did not remain there long. Less than a year later, they packed up and moved to a house Harold had bought in Croton-on-Hudson, New York, about 30 miles north of New York City. From then on, Gray was a visitor in Chicago.

Annie, too, was busy all the time. After she and Daddy had gone home from the Silos', they discovered that Mrs. Warbucks had run off to Europe with Count De Tour. Daddy missed her, but somehow didn't get around to looking for her until a year and a half later. He found her, then lost her again in a yachting accident, and she was never heard from again.

Annie, meanwhile, had wandered off with Sandy and ended up helping a poor woman feed her many children. The woman, Mrs. Pewter, sewed a red dress for Annie, the one she wore almost invariably for the next half-century. Next to her vacant eyeballs, that dress was the subject of more reader mail than any other aspect of the strip.

In the summer of 1928, Annie was nabbed by the juvenile authorities and put back with Miss Asthma. One night a fire broke out in the orphanage. Annie stayed cool and got the other children out, but she herself was trapped in the conflagration. Her badly burned body was discovered in the ruins of the orphanage by a distraught Daddy Warbucks. Through a medical miracle—again, the first of many— Annie made a full recovery and was soon off on another adventure with Sandy.

About the same time, the rival King Features Syndicate, owned by the Hearst newspaper chain, decided that if one orphan girl could be so popular in the comics, there must be room for profit with another.

"THE KID LOOKS LIKE A PANSY TO ME"

They inaugurated a strip of their own called *Little Annie Rooney*, which featured a 12-year-old girl in a tattered dress who wandered about with her little dog, Zero, as her only companion. Instead of "Leapin' lizards," Annie Rooney's litany was, "Glorioski!"

Little Annie Rooney first appeared on January 10, 1929. It was written by Brandon Walsh and drawn by a number of artists, in assorted styles, until 1931, when a young artist named Darrell McClure took it over. Although it was a blatant copycat of Gray's strips, *Annie Rooney* had a respectable subscription list—and a healthy measure of praise for its drawing and writing—until it was discontinued in 1966.

As the autumn of 1929 approached, Annie, Sandy, Daddy, Gray, and everyone else in America were blissfully unaware of the impending catastrophe that would plunge the world into misery and despair. The coming decade would bring Annie and her creator an uncommon share of blessings. The years when America endured its worst hour would be their finest.

Chapter 3

HARD TIMES

No one who lived through the Great Depression can fully describe the anguish of that time, and nobody born since then can fully comprehend the humiliations it brought to people's lives. An entire generation was scarred for life by memories of the economic disaster.

As those memories faded, there was a tendency in history books to compress the Depression into a short span: the stock market crashed in 1929 and the world was dumped into bankruptcy. In reality, the events that led up to the Crash and the economic disaster that followed occurred gradually. Many words have been used to describe how the Depression affected ordinary people; the most common and accurate one is *fear*. Uncharacteristically, Americans were a frightened people as they watched the solid structures of their society collapse before them, one after another, with the same fascination with which a silent crowd watches a burning building.

On a single day—Tuesday, October 29, 1929—as much as $74 billion (to this day, nobody knows precisely how much) was wiped out in panic selling on Wall Street. That sum represented not only the life savings of millions of people, but the resources of thousands of businesses as well. In one day, the capital base of the national economy simply disappeared.

Next came the banks. Nervous depositors lined up to withdraw their savings, only to find that the banks, too, had been "playing the market." The money was not there. Within six months after the crash, more than 1,000 banks across America had closed their doors.

HARD TIMES

Finally, the economy itself collapsed. Unemployment soared, and for the first time in the history of the United States emigration exceeded immigration: three times as many people were leaving the country as were entering it. A nation built on sweat and muscle became a nation of idle hands. Food and shelter, for so long taken for granted in a land of plenty, became the objects of everyday struggle.

Among those who were spared that struggle were Mr. and Mrs. Harold Gray. Thanks to a handsome income from the syndication of *Little Orphan Annie*, Gray and his new bride escaped the misery inflicted on so many others. If anything, they profited nicely. The strip reached the zenith of its popularity during the Thirties, when more than 500 newspapers in North America subscribed to it. The Grays' income was further enhanced when *Little Orphan Annie* became the basis for a network radio program in 1930, and for two Hollywood movies, in 1932 and 1938.

All that money made Gray, both then and now, the object of ridicule because of the conservative, pro-business dogma he took to thumping in his comic strip. There he was, sitting pretty while millions were starving and homeless, preaching to them about hard work and individual initiative.

Those who cursed him into hell and damnation, however, acted as if he'd acquired that viewpoint overnight. That was not the case. This, after all, was a man who had plowed fields with a team of horses at the age of nine, and worked his way through college digging ditches. That kind of gritty determination had brought him great success and a lot of money. No one would ever convince him that hard work wasn't the natural price to be paid for everything a person got out of life, or that mollycoddling people with a lot of help they didn't really need wasn't the best way to make them lazy.

Gray certainly wasn't the only man in America to have those opinions, but he was the only one who had a widely read daily feature in which to express them. When he got up on his soapbox, which he did more often than not from the Thirties on, he was more columnist than cartoonist.

All over America, many people who were unable to afford their mortgage payments or rent were forced from their homes and were living in shantytowns that sprang up on the outskirts of every major city. Those were called "Hoovervilles," a sarcastic reference to President Herbert Hoover, who was widely blamed (and still is in some quarters) for doing nothing to help those in desperate need. The President refused to ask Congress for direct relief from the federal treasury, saying it would "injure the spiritual responses of the American people." Gray undoubtedly shared that view, and was sym-

23

pathetic to the many businessmen who were as bewildered by events as anyone else. He thought they were getting a raw deal and Gray wanted to tell their side of the story. He did it through their man in his comic strip and, increasingly, his own alter ego—Daddy Warbucks.

But first he had to get people's attention. So in 1931, along with the rest of the country, Daddy went broke.

"I knew business was bad, but I figured we were big and strong enough to go through any depression," Warbucks remarked one day to his chief accountant, who'd brought him the bad news from the ledgers. But with typical optimism, Daddy rolled up his sleeves and burned the midnight oil, working to turn things around. "The country is sound. Good times are here," he remarked cheerfully, which was what so many readers of *Little Orphan Annie* wanted so fervently to hear. "Our business must not be too far gone to be saved. I'll find a way out yet." He didn't want to worry Annie, so he kept from her just how bad things were.

Aside from Herbert Hoover, bankers were the least popular people of 1931. Many banks had failed, leaving their depositors penniless. So it was predictable that when Warbucks went to see his old and dear friend Tom Bullion, he, too, would find that bankers regarded loan applications, even from old and dear friends, as "merely a matter of business." Warbucks was turned down.

Daddy was then beset by all the dark figures who thrived in the Depression—"creditors . . . jackals with papers to serve . . . the customary collection of coyotes." One by one, his servants slipped away. "They all think Daddy is goin' broke and they're afraid they won't get paid," Annie told Sandy with touching naiveté. " 'Magine that? Why, with all his money, how could Daddy ever go broke?"

That was the disbelieving voice of America. Two years after the stock market crashed, many people still couldn't quite grasp what was happening around them.

"When you're doing well everyone is your pal," Warbucks reflected bitterly to himself in his cold, lonely mansion. "It's when the hard luck hits that you can really tell the wheat from the chaff. It's easy to be a friend to someone who is doing well and who pays the bills. It's not so easy to be a friend when it's expensive."

With the limousines repossessed and the telephone shut off, Daddy was finally evicted from his home, as were so many others in real life. And like other breadwinners, suddenly broke and wondering why, Daddy blamed himself for his troubles and anguished over how to break the news to Annie:

"I've got to tell her. She has so much faith in me. And now she'll find out I've been just a common sap."

HARD TIMES

Working up his nerve, he finally blurted it out: "I'm a failure, Annie. I did the best I know how. I was not dishonest. But I have lost everything, even lost *you*, I suppose. Why, you can't care for an old duffer like me anymore now. I deserve it, Annie, but it's been mighty hard to tell you."

His worry had been for nothing. He had seriously underestimated Annie's devotion to him. "Is *that* all?" she said, hugging him. "I knew somethin' was wrong, but I figgered it must be somethin' real *bad. Shux!* What's losin' yer dough? Lots o' folks go bust. I've been poor before. It's not so bad."

How *that* speech must have gone over at many a breakfast table!

With just a few dollars in their pockets and only the clothes on their backs, Annie, Sandy, and Daddy started walking toward the city, and got a lift.

"Mighty decent of that truck driver to offer us a ride," Daddy said appreciatively.

"Poor folks are most always pretty good-hearted," Annie assured him.

When they reached the city, they were on Annie's turf. Her resourcefulness got them a cheap but comfortable room, and Daddy began scanning the want ads for a job. Like millions of others, he found out that landing a new job was far from easy. He began by inquiring after an executive position, but was soon reduced to looking for "any sort of laboring job." Even that seemed out of the question, though.

Warbucks' reflections on the situation could have been spoken by almost anyone: "I always said any man who had his health and his two hands could get work if he *wanted* to work. Huh! What a sap I was! I have no union card and no trade. I applied at a dozen different places for a job as a clerk or a bookkeeper. Bet I walked twenty miles today and climbed a hundred flights of stairs. But I'll keep at it. I won't give up. I'll land a job."

Just when they were down to the last of their food, Daddy did find work as a day laborer, bringing home three dollars a day. After a couple of weeks, though, he was laid off. In the meantime, Annie started working for their groceries at the local market, where her cheerful industriousness impressed the owner. That made Daddy's despair complete: "Great scott! Has it come to this? Warbucks practically supported by a little girl? What's the matter with me? Why can't I get going? I can't seem to get or hold even the simplest kind of job. And now Annie, whom I should be taking care of, is earning the very food we eat. I'm just a fumbling old misfit!"

Like other men used to being the family provider, Warbucks

couldn't adjust to being dependent on a dependent. Annie came home one day to find him gone, leaving only a note saying he'd be back when he'd "made good." That, too, was something that happened to many families in real life.

But Gray was not content to put Daddy through any kind of normal wringer. He really piled it on. Warbucks got a job driving a truck, but then went blind after a collision. He spent a long time in the hospital charity ward, where the doctors told him he'd never see again, and when he left there he found lodging in a flophouse run by a midget named Bill.

Just as surely as the darkest hour comes before dawn, though, the characters in *Little Orphan Annie* always made a comeback. Confiding his true identity to his new friend Bill, Warbucks set out to recover his lost fortune. Learning that his ruin was caused by an old nemesis, J.J. Shark, Daddy disguised himself behind a beard and dark glasses and, using Bill's savings as a small stake, started to rebuild his business empire and turn the tables on Shark.

He didn't want Annie to know that he'd gone blind, but he was worried how she was getting along without him. And when he sent her $100 in cash in a letter purportedly mailed from far away, her ensuing trip to the local bank illustrated the skepticism that most people felt then toward banks and bankers.

"Gee, yuh can't be too careful in pickin' a bank these days," she told Sandy. "I don't want to put my dough in any bank that's likely to fold up." When she got to the teller's window, she demanded reassurance that her money would be safe, that she could withdraw it anytime she wanted, and that she'd be paid interest on it. That kind of talk wouldn't have been necessary a few years earlier, but with banks closing their doors left and right, depositors were justifiably edgy about handing over their hard-earned cash.

When Daddy learned of her thriftiness, he put another $5,000 into her account anonymously. That brought a phalanx of salesmen, hucksters, con artists, and snake-oil peddlers to Annie's doorstep, offering to sell her everything from accident insurance to "surefire" stock deals and business partnerships. Annie turned them all down cold. Like most other Americans, she was determined to hold onto what she had; the get-rich-quick schemes of the Twenties were still a bitter memory for everyone.

Inevitably, Daddy outmaneuvered J.J. Shark and sent him to the poorhouse, in the process becoming a billionaire once more. But he still could not bring himself to face Annie so long as he was blind. So off he sailed to Europe and the one-in-a-million chance that the doctors there could restore his sight.

HARD TIMES

The sequence in which Warbucks lost and then regained his fortune lasted nearly a year—long even by Gray's standards. The readers of *Little Orphan Annie* could take some small amount of cheer in the fact that Warbucks, at least, had made it. Unfortunately, he was one of the very few.

Being as much or more dramatist as cartoonist, Gray kept his strip from growing monotonous by branching off occasionally into subplots. Annie's experiences working at the grocery store comprised one, and her adventures with a couple of con artists were another. A third introduced a new character who would become a staple of the Sunday color page and stayed with Gray until his death: Maw Green.

The proprietor of the rooming house where Annie, Sandy, and Daddy had gone to live after Daddy went broke, Maw was a middle-aged widow with a hard shell but a soft spot in her heart for an underdog. It's even possible to think of her as the kind of woman Annie might have become if Gray had ever allowed her to grow up.

Maw's kindness toward Annie and Sandy was rewarded when a "rich uncle in the old country"—again, it was Warbucks acting anonymously—died and left her a tidy sum. His faith in her basic virtue was borne out when she passed up the chance to buy a lot of fancy things, and instead invested the money in a modest house in a nice neighborhood. "In spite of riches, Annie, I'll never be a fine lady. I'm still just old Maw Green, and I know it. Society! Bah! I prefer the society of a good dog to the society of a lot of money-worshipers that'd smirk in my face and sneer at my back. I'll have contentment. That's more than lots of rich folks."

Daddy, his sight miraculously restored, came back in time for Christmas of 1931. Gray had gotten into the habit of plotting out *Little Orphan Annie* by writing, in longhand, in yearly appointment books, the dialogue that would be spoken in each day's four-panel installment. Those books, later donated to Boston University, were also filled with sketches of new characters, the names he made up for each, and some random observations. Gray was given to rumination at year's end, both publicly in the comic strip, and privately in his diaries. The entry for Monday, December 28, 1931, reads: "Sort of dull between Xmas and New Year—good time to sit down and quietly go over past year. Its blessings and disappointments. Triumphs and mistakes. Warbucks sure has had a taste of about everything. All fine now."

With the basic cast of *Little Orphan Annie* well established, Gray felt no compunction about moving new characters in and out of the never-ending action. In early 1932, for instance, Daddy got to thinking that it might be best for Annie if she were part of a "normal" family. He decided to get married again and did, to an ex-showgirl named Trixie. She turned out to be a classic gold digger, though, and within a few months the marriage went sour. Trixie scooted off to a crooked lawyer and, together, they hatched a scheme to soak Warbucks for some fat alimony. Daddy tried to patch things up by taking her on a long cruise, from which he returned alone. Like so many other people who crossed Daddy over the years, she disappeared without a trace and was never spoken of again.

Two other new characters who arrived in the mid-Thirties, though, became permanent fixtures of *Little Orphan Annie*: Punjab and the Asp. A turbaned East Indian of giant proportions and a dapper, sinister-looking man of vaguely Asian origin, Punjab and the Asp served as Warbucks' bodyguards and, on occasion, his assassins. Their strong suit was making Daddy's enemies disappear.

Punjab possessed a "magic cloak" that could make the people it was thrown over vanish into thin air. Where had they gone? Annie wanted to know after its first demonstration. "Who can say?" Punjab replied with a small shrug. Sometimes he told her they had gone "to travel with the Magi." Always, though, they were gone for good and would "bother no mortal ever again." Under less genteel circumstances—for instance, in the hand-to-hand fighting Daddy engaged in once in a while—Punjab would brandish the huge sword that always hung from his waist sash and mow down his opponents. It was a gruesome spectacle.

The Asp, on the other hand, was a wily creature—a coiled snake who was as dangerous as his name implied. His methods of eliminating Daddy's foes were less visible than Punjab's, but no less effective.

With the introduction of Punjab and the Asp, *Little Orphan Annie* took on the violent, merciless tone that would later exasperate even Gray's friends and supporters.

In November 1932, Franklin D. Roosevelt was elected President of the United States in a landslide vote. By the time he took the oath of office the following March, America had hit bottom. Something on the order of 17 million people were out of work, six million were on the dole, banks everywhere were closing their doors, and army units were quietly taking up posts near the larger cities because the situation had become so desperate that a second American revolution was not entirely out of the question.

On his first day in office, Roosevelt ordered the 19,000 banks that were still functioning to close for four days. The "bank holiday" gave federal examiners time to go over their books, but, more important, it provided a breathing space for panic-stricken depositors. FDR summoned Congress into an emergency session that lasted 100 days; when it was over, the United States had indeed undergone a second revolution, but a peaceful one. The President demanded and got new laws that gave the federal government a much bigger role in regulating banking, farming, industry, and labor. He called it the "New Deal" and it had many admirers. But it also made him some enemies, people who saw the intrusion of the government into the affairs of private enterprise as nothing short of socialism. They had unprintable names for it, and for Roosevelt, and they bitterly, though unsuccessfully, opposed them both.

Gray was an enemy of the New Deal. He regarded such programs as Social Security as a subversion of America's time-honored work ethic. And though he ran no corporation, he had at his disposal an instrument that no amount of money could buy: daily exposure in hundreds of newspapers from coast to coast.

In 1931, *Little Orphan Annie* was far and away the single most popular comic strip in the New York *News*, and in many of the other papers in which it appeared. Anyone who discounted the clout wielded by a comic strip could read what the famous columnist Heywood Broun wrote at the time in *The New Republic* magazine: "These strips, whether we like it or not, constitute the proletarian novels of America. They are scanned by millions. To those who cannot read the long words of literature, the comic strip is extremely valuable. To those who cannot read any, it is indispensable."

Soon, Annie and Sandy were facing danger not only from the familiar pack of gangsters, crooked politicians, and common criminals, but were also victimized by social workers, do-gooders, bureaucrats, and other New Dealers. As depicted in *Little Orphan Annie*, they were rigid interlopers who were sapping Americans of their natural resilience and dedication to hard work.

Gray was prepared to put Daddy Warbucks up on the cross, if necessary, to perish for the sins of capitalism. He got his chance in early 1934, and took it: Warbucks became the object of government persecution, at the same time a flesh-and-blood demigod of capitalism named Samuel J. Insull was suffering at the hands of government prosecutors.

The saga of Samuel Insull's fall from power and prestige, now just a footnote to history, was one of the most widely publicized spectacles of the Depression years. It was an American success story gone wrong.

A bright, ambitious young man who'd grown up in the slums of

London, Insull became Thomas Edison's private secretary at the age of 21. Having learned the technical and financial aspects of electrical power from the master himself, Insull was made president of the Chicago Edison Company in 1892 and over the next four decades constructed, largely with small investors' money, a huge utility empire that literally lit up the Midwest. He lived on an estate outside of Chicago that encompassed more than 4,000 acres, where he raised Swiss cattle and English horses and lived in a mansion with gold-plated bathroom fixtures and a private post office. If ever there was a real man whose wealth equaled Oliver Warbucks' fictional fortune, it was Samuel Insull.

The Insull utility empire survived the first spasms of the Depression with little outward sign of damage. Bankers continued to lend him any amount of money he requested—at the same time they were refusing to buy tax warrants from the City of Chicago.

But like all megalomaniacs, Insull was not quite as smart as he thought he was, and in 1930 he was outmaneuvered badly in the stock market by Cleveland industrialist Cyrus Eaton. Insull was put over a barrel to the tune of $63 million at the same time he was working to replace the infusion of small investors' money that had been wiped out in the Crash. The banks no longer had any money to lend him. He turned to Wall Street, which floated him a short-term loan, but by then his house of cards was already falling. In April 1932 the Insull empire went into bankruptcy, and it was revealed that it consisted mostly of worthless paper. Peeling back layer after layer of his interlocking network, investigators found that Insull's business dealings over the years had become so complex that even he no longer understood them.

Insull resigned his posts in 85 companies and sailed to Europe. He left behind him the largest business failure in U.S. history: thousands of little people who had entrusted their life savings to him had lost $750 million. They demanded retribution, and five months after he'd resigned and the full extent of the disaster became known, Insull was indicted by a Cook County grand jury on charges of embezzlement and larceny.

The Illinois state attorney demanded that he come back and stand trial. Instead, he left Paris for Turin, Italy. But when American authorities sought him out there, they discovered he had fled to Greece, which had no extradition treaty with the United States. In the meantime, he had been indicted in Chicago again, for mail fraud. Under pressure from the American ambassador, the Greek foreign minister ordered Insull to leave the country. He boarded a tramp steamer in March 1933 and vanished into the Aegean Sea.

HARD TIMES

The same month, Gray kicked the legs out from under Warbucks. In a loud soliloquy, Daddy had proclaimed his intention to pay his fair share of taxes, as was the duty of every citizen. But a trusted employee absconded with the money set aside to pay Warbucks' taxes, and he was immediately indicted by the Justice Department for tax evasion.

"Is this the answer to ambition?" Daddy lamented. "The reward for giving every ounce of thought and effort for a lifetime?" The parallel between Warbucks and Insull was unmistakable.

As was his habit, Gray painted the ensuing trial in black-and-white terms. The prosecutor was an unscrupulous district attorney named Phil O. Bluster. He confided to his cronies that he knew perfectly well that Warbucks was innocent but must be convicted because "the voters will eat that up." Equipped with false evidence, Bluster prepared to rake Daddy over the legal coals. The distraught ex-billionaire remarked sadly, "Because a few men have gained riches by crooked dealing, Bluster and his kind scream that all rich men are dishonest rascals."

Meanwhile, back in the real world, Insull had unsuccessfully sought asylum in Turkey. He was arrested and handed over to American authorities, who placed him on a ship bound for New York. It was six months between the time the ship docked and Insull's trial in Chicago began. That gave the public relations man Insull's son had hired plenty of time to remodel the old man's image. He was to be depicted as a well-meaning but unlucky man who was determined to accept sole responsibility for his past mistakes.

Correspondingly, in the panels of *Little Orphan Annie* Warbucks was brought to trial before an obviously hostile jury that consisted of several radicals and the worst kind of creep that Gray could imagine—a college professor. If there was any doubt that this would be a kangaroo court, it was removed when one juror remarked to another before the trial even began: "Yeh, he's guilty. Why try him?"

At that, New Deal advocate (and later U.S. Senator) Richard Neuberger could no longer contain himself. In an article published in *The New Republic* in July 1934, under the title "Hooverism in the Funnies," Neuberger wrote a scathing attack on Gray's satire of the Insull trial:

Noting sarcastically that *Little Orphan Annie* was distributed by "that palladium of American democracy, the Chicago *Tribune*," Neuberger said it was "inevitable that the strip should eventually be used in the current crusade to create martyrs out of millionaires and unscrupulous demagogues out of vigilant district attorneys and militant Senators.

31

"From 1925 to 1934 there was no more lovable or more consistently fortunate comic-strip character than Daddy Warbucks," Neuberger went on, then cited Daddy's recent reversals as part of Gray's sinister campaign to do "heroic service in the cause of Andrew W. Mellon (Hoover's Treasury Secretary), Samuel Insull and other persecuted philanthropists."

He pointed out the parallels between the real-life trial of Insull and the pen-and-ink sufferings of Warbucks. "At the current writing, Daddy Warbucks is on trial for cheating the government out of its taxes," Neuberger wrote. "Of course, everyone knows he is not guilty; he is being railroaded by agitating politicians, malcontents and dangerous college professors. And Mr. Gray's clever cartoons, handled by the Chicago *Tribune* syndicate, are being distributed to 135 daily and 100 Sunday [Neuberger's figures were too low] papers, and thence to millions of citizens, while Samuel Insull awaits trial for the collapse of his utilities empire at the hands of a government whose President is influenced by insidious university pedagogues and whose insurgent legislators wear shoestring ties."

The public relations man hired for Samuel Insull did a splendid job. By the time the jury retired to debate the verdict only a child molester would have been able to find him guilty. He was acquitted on all charges in that and two subsequent trials. Warbucks, however, was convicted and sent to jail. He was eventually reprieved by the governor after Bluster and his cronies were exposed, and his name was cleared.

If Gray had been stung by the criticism that came his way during the Insull-Warbucks sequence, the pain faded fast. But only a few months later, in June 1935, good old capitalism à la Warbucks was under attack again, this time by the marauding hordes of organized labor.

The Thirties was a time of great labor turmoil that pitted Walter Reuther and John L. Lewis against Henry Ford and U.S. Steel. Businessmen saw labor activism as a dangerous threat to their own existence, and, as part of their overreaction, common thugs were hired as plant guards and given implied permission to physically beat obstinate union organizers into submission.

Not surprisingly, Gray took up the businessman's cause with a sequence that began midway through 1935. In it, Warbucks befriended an old beggar, who turned out to be a brilliant, eccentric inventor named Eli Eon. A substance he'd concocted, known as "eonite," was the ultimate industrial product. "It will revolutionize the civilized world," Daddy assured Annie. "It's transparent as glass, but will take any color. It's many times stronger than steel. Neither acid, heat, time nor weather affects eonite in the least. Eonite will be used to replace everything built or used by man, from buildings to dishes. The nation that possesses eonite will have nothing to fear from foreign foes. Oh, it's great stuff, Annie."

Impressed, Annie replied, "Gee, now that people know about it, other folks will want it, too." But Daddy, an ardent patriot, wasn't about to share his plum with the rest of the world and vowed to produce eonite "for the war needs of my own nation only, and at no profit to myself."

Warbucks was also cast in the light of industrial philanthropy. Once his factory was set up and running, he announced, his first order of business would be to not only hire thousands of unemployed workers, but to give them all "a substantial raise—that's only fair." That particular utterance appeared in a strip headlined, "The Square Deal," Gray's blunt reply to FDR's game plan.

In the unlikely event that somebody might have missed the ten-ton point of it all, Warbucks expounded further on the blessings to society that eonite would bring: "In a few years all shacks and slums will be eliminated. Living costs will fall. National wealth will increase tremendously. Those with the least will live better than our rich today."

Daddy's dedication to bettering the lot of all mankind was positively heartrending. As he burned the midnight oil in his office, the golden knight of free enterprise consoled himself with the thought that "a *few* men *have* to work hard and take chances and battle heavy odds and worry nights so that millions may have that 'fuller life'—instead of *every* day off *without pay*." In retrospect, words like that seem unbearably self-serving, but at the time they were printed, there really were many people on involuntary unpaid vacations who would have welcomed something like eonite.

Things were definitely looking rosy as the Warbucks conglomerate got tooled up and the first batch of the miracle substance started down the assembly line. But anyone who had read *Little Orphan Annie* must have suspected that just as things were beginning to run along smoothly, trouble was surely on the way. It arrived in the person of J. Slugg, yet another of Warbucks' rivals. Naturally, he was jealous of Daddy's impending bonanza and wanted to steal the formula for eonite for himself. He enlisted the aid of his own bought-and-paid-for public official, a silver-tongued bit of slime named Claude Claptrap. Having failed in his attempt to stir up labor trouble—Warbucks' factory, of course, was a nonunion shop and his workers were so happy and content that they tarred and feathered the union agitators sent in to organize them—Slugg then unleashed Claptrap's oratory on the masses.

Eonite "should belong to the *pee-pul*," Claptrap told the large gatherings that suddenly materialized out of nowhere; Warbucks was a "beast of prey" who was selfishly keeping eonite for his own personal profit. Within a matter of days, Claptrap had succeeded in turning Warbucks' happy workers into a violent, ugly mob.

Daddy's advisors urged him to launch a propaganda campaign to counter Claptrap's lies, but Gray, mirroring the impotence felt by businessmen "victimized" by the New Deal, wouldn't allow it. "I'm a worker," he declared. "A producer. A businessman. I'm not a cheap politician. What did any politician *ever* produce?" That started him on a ripping tirade: "Suppose a mob *should* destroy the plant and deliver it into Slugg's hands? That would mean ruin and slavery for the whole human race, instead of the prosperity and happiness that I am trying to bring to all."

"That's true," a subordinate murmured reverently.

With the mob crashing through the factory gates, the plant guards begged Warbucks for permission to fire into the crowd. But the philosopher-king of capitalism refused. "No—I'll not allow one innocent person to be shot down. Let them burn it. We can rebuild a plant, but no one can restore a human life." Gray wasn't about to let FDR and his New Dealers hold a monopoly on compassion.

The National Guard was called out, but it arrived too late to save the factory, which was destroyed by the rampaging mob. Eli Eon and his formula for eonite also perished in the conflagration. Warbucks knew whose fault it really was: "I can't blame the mob. Say rather that he was killed by the irresponsible hate-makers; demagogues seeking applause and votes—the rabble-rousers—that's where the real blame lies."

Too late, the workers realized they had smashed the means of their own prosperity. A handful of them, idle and out of work once again, came upon one of the leaders of the mob. Warbucks watched from a distance as they beat the man to a bloody pulp, and reflected on "how quickly public sentiment can change when people stop dreaming and really come awake."

Not surprisingly, the eonite sequence brought howls of protest from organized labor and the New Dealers. The Huntington *Herald Dispatch*, in the heart of West Virginia's coal-mining country, dropped *Little Orphan Annie* with a front-page editorial that denounced Gray's strip as "the vehicle for studied, veiled and alarmingly vindictive propaganda." A subsequent article in the September 1935 *New Republic* applauding the paper's action further castigated

Gray for preaching that "all reform legislation of the Roosevelt administration, and all attempts to extend union organizations, were no more than the tricks of one set of capitalists to ruin another set," and that "those who now rule industry are good and kindly, and that their rivals are evil."

The magazine noted with satisfaction that the editor of the *Herald Dispatch* had received a speedy telegram from the Tribune syndicate that read: ORPHAN ANNIE ARTIST ORDERED STOP EDITORIALIZING AND HAS ALREADY STARTED NEW SERIES. FEEL SURE YOU WILL LIKE IT. That was the first time the syndicate pinned Gray's ears back. It would not be the last.

The heavy-handed polemics of *Little Orphan Annie* were counter-weighted by refinements in the strip that brought it to its creative peak during the Thirties. Its immense popularity was demonstrated time and time again by the continuing avalanche of letters from readers that filled Gray's mailbox. One special communiqué arrived in January 1933 during a sequence in which Annie had become separated from Sandy and was searching for him far and wide. It was a telegram from Dearborn, Michigan, that read: PLEASE DO ALL YOU CAN TO HELP ANNIE FIND SANDY. STOP. WE ARE ALL INTERESTED. HENRY FORD.

Gray's skills as an artist and as a dramatist became highly developed during this period. "There is some question whether I ever really learned to draw," he once joked about himself. But even those who never much admired his style will admit that his dexterity with his characters and backgrounds became classic in the early Thirties. Annie, Sandy, and Daddy were smooth and distinctive. The panels were well proportioned, with a studied look about them. Gray developed a shading technique well suited to the sinister, shadowy mood of his story lines.

The plots became more and more intricate—a difficult feat to pull off because some subscribers bought only the Monday-through-Saturday daily strips, while others read only the color Sunday episode, which often began with a homily drawn from Aristotle or Shakespeare or Abe Lincoln. That required Gray to build his continuity so that it would make sense to readers who saw only the daily or only the Sunday strips. Inevitably, Monday was a rehashing day. Gray handled it deftly.

One particular sequence, which occupied most of 1938, is commonly regarded as the absolute crest of *Little Orphan Annie*. It was a detective story as suspenseful and well-told as any ever put into prose by Raymond Chandler or Dashiell Hammett.

It began the week before Christmas 1937. "I got the idea when I read Hawthorne's *House of the Seven Gables*," Gray explained at the time. "It isn't *House of the Seven Gables*, but the book fermented the germ of an idea. Annie and Sandy were tossed out in the snow by a truck driver, who didn't want to be caught kidnaping. She found Rose Chance in the snow with a baby. It happened on Christmas, and though probably no one thought of it, it might have been the Virgin Mary parable."

Annie, Sandy, and Rose Chance and her baby boy landed in a small town, where they were taken in by a kind widow, Mrs. Alden. Annie helped her save her house from mortgage foreclosure by the town scrooge, named Uriah Gudge. One day a mysterious one-legged tramp showed up, and Mrs. Alden let him sleep in the woodshed in exchange for a few chores. Unknown to anyone, Old Shanghai Peg had been first mate on the *Cathay Kate*, the ship captained by Mrs. Alden's late husband, Caleb. Shanghai had arrived to avenge the death of Captain Alden 30 years earlier at the hands of . . . Uriah Gudge. When Gudge suddenly disappeared, the sheriff and townspeople believed that Shanghai had murdered him and buried his body at the bottom of a well before skipping town in the middle of the night. For several weeks, the sheriff's men dug slowly down the well, as Gray brought the suspense to an unbearable level. Some readers couldn't hold on until the end.

"My dear Mr. Gray: We can't believe that you are going to allow good old Shanghai to be thought a murderer, even by implication," wrote a woman from Arlington, Massachusetts. "Please clear this up shortly—Old Gudge could have committed suicide, or even fallen into the old well. But Shanghai? Never!"

Another reader in Aurora, Colorado, sent an angry letter to the Denver *Post*, demanding that the paper stop printing *Little Orphan Annie* until the Shanghai story ended. "As a father, grandfather, and something of a student of ethics and psychology, I want to protest against the continuance of the Orphan Annie strip in your (our) paper."

He feared the story would teach children that "when a good man knows that a certain man is unworthy to live, the proper thing to do is to secretly put him at the bottom of a well (dead, or alive?), fill the well with dirt, add some concrete, and cover that with sod. . . . I do not think that the *Post* wishes to even suggest such flaunting of law, order and judicial procedure. But the Orphan Annie strip is most effectively drilling it into the minds of our children." And he added: "Its author seems to me to always identify virtue with deep cunning and brute force."

But when the bottom of the well was finally reached, the sheriff's men—and millions of readers—discovered not the body of Uriah Gudge, but a small metal chest that contained his handwritten confession to the murder of Captain Caleb Alden and the theft of his money and property. It was a dénouement that ranked alongside that of any great murder mystery.

The Shanghai story was the most carefully crafted and brilliantly executed sequence ever written and drawn in Gray's 54 years on the strip.

That same year, 1938, Gray and his wife moved out of their house in Croton-on-Hudson to Westport, Connecticut, then a small hamlet in affluent Fairfield County. The mansion they leased was fit for Daddy Warbucks. It was pretty fancy digs for the likes of Annie and Sandy, though, in the opinion of a reporter for the Bridgeport *Post* who visited there.

"Though you have seen them through the windows of the comic page in rags, indigent of worldly goods and rich only in a simple but hard-boiled philosophy, right now they are more than comfortably ensconced in a magnificent 17-acre estate on a quiet hilltop in Greenacre Lane with their creator, Harold Gray," wrote the reporter, Eileen Wilson, in a Sunday feature story on February 20, 1938. "No poor but honest hovel is this stone house of Norman architecture, but a pretentious residence called 'Rockledge' with endless rooms, well-manicured lawns and drives, and a coveted view of Long Island Sound."

The Grays had become wealthy during the Depression, and moving into a mansion in Connecticut was their way of putting on the Ritz. But it didn't last long. It must not have been comfortable for two people who were being supported by an orphan. The following year, they bought a less ostentatious house in a "beautiful, exclusive section" a few miles away, according to another Bridgeport *Post* article. The Grays lived in four houses during their 30 years in the Westport vicinity, each one more modest than the one before. Gray may have thought like Daddy Warbucks, but he didn't want to live like him.

Chapter 4

THAT LITTLE CHATTERBOX

It was remarkably easy to locate huge numbers of American children during the decade between 1930 and 1940. At 5:45 P.M. EST, all you had to do was find the nearest radio, and the chances were good that you would find at least one youngster, ears perked up, listening to *Adventure Time With Orphan Annie.*

Radio had grown by leaps and bounds during the Twenties, and by the end of the decade had become a national mass medium with nearly 700 stations broadcasting into some 14 million American households. Early attempts to keep advertising off the airwaves had failed, and commercial networks blossomed as companies eagerly sought radio programs to sponsor.

One of them was Ovaltine, a company in Villa Park, Illinois, that manufactures a powdered malt-flavored milk supplement that has become synonymous with the term "malted milk." Like other sponsors, Ovaltine wanted a radio show that would attract potential purchasers of its product—in this case, children—and then encourage them to actually go out and buy it. Annie was perfect.

Ovaltine obtained the paid permission of Gray and the Tribune syndicate to use the character, and in December 1930 *Little Orphan Annie* went on the air, broadcast from the studios of WGN in Chicago, then owned by the Tribune Company. The voice of Annie belonged to 10-year-old Shirley Bell, already a veteran radio performer. The stories, similar in tone to Gray's, were written by Frank

Dahm. They were set in the fictional town of Tompkins Corners, where Annie and Sandy were living with the Silos (the same couple whose brief custody of Annie back in 1925 had caused such a ruckus). The radio scripts deviated from Gray's handling of the strip chiefly in the presence of Joe Corntassle, Annie's constant companion, who was played first by child actor Allen Baruck, and later by a future famous singer named Mel Tormé.

The show proved to be so popular that it was picked up by NBC's Blue Network (which later became ABC) six months after it began. It held an audience of children estimated at six million entranced five evenings a week, from 5:45 to 6 P.M., EST.

In its early days, the show's opening and closing signature was a theme song written by WGN's music director, Del Owens. The tune and words that went with it were carved indelibly into the minds of the show's juvenile listeners:

> Who's that little chatterbox?
> The one with pretty auburn locks?
> Cute little she,
> It's Little Orphan Annie.
>
> Bright eyes, always on the go,
> There's a sort of healthiness handy.
> Mite size, cheeks a-rosy glow,
> If you want to know,
> "Arf!" says Sandy.
>
> Always wears a sunny smile,
> Now, wouldn't it be worth your while
> If you could be
> Like Little Orphan Annie?

That theme song was so well known that more than three decades later, a humorous article written by Richard Gehman for the *Saturday Review* of July 12, 1969, suggested that there was easy money to be made at any cocktail party simply by challenging the nearest middle-aged person to sing the words to the *Little Orphan Annie* theme song.

"*All* people during that period—budding delinquents, safecrackers, stock market manipulators, or whatever—listened to 'Little Orphan Annie,' " Gehman wrote. In his scheme, the bet would be taken, of course, but after happily chanting the first two lines, the pigeon would stop cold, a victim of aging memory, and have to fork over the stake.

Gehman, revealing himself for all the world as a rabid Annie aficionado, went on to cite the inaccuracies in the lyrics: Annie was never a "chatterbox"; her eyes, contrary to being "bright," were "as expressionless as a pair of small ironstone dishes"; Sandy "explained absolutely nothing by saying 'Arf!' No dog in the annals of dog history has ever said 'arf,' any more than one has ever said 'bow wow' "; and it "wouldn't be worth anybody's while if he or she could be like Little Orphan Annie. Disaster was always imminent in her life, or sorrow at Daddy's frequent disappearances, which in my view occurred only because he wished to get the hell away from his ward."

The song, like nearly everything about Annie, was eminently spoofable. In 1958, writer Larry Siegel parodied the theme song's lyrics as part of a song-sheet satire published in the short-lived humor magazine *Humbug*. He called his "Little Orphan Nannie":

> Who's that little chatterbox?
> The one with Nova Scotia lox?
> Whom can it be?
> It's Little Orphan Nannie.
>
> Bright eyes, pimple on her nose,
> Everywhere she goes
> "Hic!" says Brandy.
>
> Always wears a reddish cloak,
> C'mon and give her neck a choke.
> It's all for free,
> Choke Little Orphan Nannie.

Often, ridicule is as sincere a form of flattery as imitation. The fact that the words to that song were so clearly remembered so many years later showed not only the staying power of childhood impressions, but the fact that kids growing up in the Thirties couldn't escape the presence of Annie any more easily than later generations of children could elude Snoopy.

After going network, the program's name was changed to *Adventure Time With Orphan Annie*, and the theme song was played on a studio organ, without lyrics.

"It's adventure time, with Orphan Annie!" was the show's new signature, spoken by announcer Pierre André over a chorus of telegraph signals, steamship horns, an airplane droning overhead, and a distant train whistle.

But before the nightly adventures of Annie and Joe Corntassle got underway, there was a lengthy plug from the makers of Ovaltine for whatever premium they happened to be giving away at the time. Ovaltine gave away more premiums on its radio shows, *Orphan*

Annie and *Captain Midnight*, than any other radio sponsor. Entire warehouses of paraphernalia—shake-up mugs that made "a picnic out of every meal," identification tags "like real soldiers and aviators wear," buttons, photos, games, masks, pins, rings, badges, bandannas, booklets, bracelets, coins, cutouts and maps—were shipped out to listeners who sent in a dime (or nickel, quarter, etc.) that had to be "wrapped in a metal foil seal from under the lid of a can of Ovaltine, or the new chocolate-flavored Ovaltine," per Monsieur André's instructions.

Among the most cherished of those trinkets were the "decoder" rings and badges that were in the sole possession of the members of Radio Orphan Annie's "Secret Society." The membership consisted of anyone who sent away for a decoder, which enabled the user to translate such important messages as "s-e-n-d h-e-l-p" or "s-a-n-d-y i-s s-a-f-e."

Long after the show went off the air, Ovaltine continued to receive requests for some of the 75 different premium items associated with Annie's show. In 1969, a letter arrived at Villa Park from a man in Mayfield Heights, Ohio, containing an ancient magazine clipping that advertised a shaker featuring "new and *different* colored pictures of Orphan Annie and Sandy on it." Enclosed was a dime dutifully wrapped in the aluminum seal from under the lid of a can of Ovaltine. Ovaltine returned the dime, and since the shaker requested had long since disappeared, sent along containers of both flavors of Ovaltine instead.

At one time, hundreds of thousands of premiums given away by Ovaltine during the 10 years it sponsored *Orphan Annie* could be found in bureau drawers all across America. Over the years, however, they became scarce and the ones still around now fetch pretty fancy prices as collectors' items. An original ceramic mug, embossed with the picture of a smiling Annie holding a mug herself and saying "Dija ever taste anything so good as Ovaltine? And it's *good for* yuh, too!" has sold for almost $50. Some of the other cups, rings, and badges are also worth many times their original prices. It's hard to say which Orphan Annie premium is *the* most valuable, but it might be one of the 25 real watches that were given away in 1931 as prizes in a word-building contest.

Ovaltine keeps its own large collection of Annie radio premiums in a museumlike setting at its Villa Park headquarters, under the watchful eyes of Lyle Bergmann. Bergmann is the company's manager of customer service and an authority on the radio show, the comic strip, and Gray's years as a resident of the neighboring town of Lombard.

To commemorate its 50th "Annie-versary" in 1981, Ovaltine

issued a limited-edition (24,000) offering of ceramic mugs with a picture of Annie and Sandy, and a 22-carat gold rim. Anyone planning to wrap a dime inside a foil seal and sending away for it was living strictly in Nostalgialand, though. For one thing, Ovaltine had long since changed its packaging to glass jars with screw-on lids, so the proof of purchase had become the jar's paper label. For another, the new mug cost $5.95.

Shirley Bell, who had to beat out 500 other children for the coveted radio role of Annie, held it for the nine and a half years the show originated at WGN. "I earned $50 a week at first," she told a *Chicago* Today interviewer in June 1970, pulling out a photostated copy of her first paycheck as proof. "I was working when no one in our family had a job during the Depression. When I finished in 1940, I was making $145."

She later married a Chicago businessman, raised three daughters, and wound up using her trained voice to record textbooks for the blind. Her recollections of the days when she played Annie on the radio had a divided tone.

"In addition to Annie, I played Sandy much of the time because I was able to whine. Someone else would growl, somebody else would bark. Sandy was always in three parts," she told a Chicago *Tribune* interviewer.

"I sometimes worked with a temperature and laryngitis. Once they rewrote the script around me. Of course, my pay was docked. Business is business," she told a reporter for another Chicago paper.

And here's a revelation: "I never drank Ovaltine. I wasn't particularly fond of the malt taste, and besides, I didn't need it. I was a very fat child."

A radio listener poll taken in 1937 found *Orphan Annie* to be tops among kids between the ages of five and eight, and a close second to *The Lone Ranger* among the nine-to-14 set.

"Just as in the newspaper page, Annie shared many scrapes with the munitions king Daddy Warbucks," wrote Chris Steinbrunner, editor of *The Encyclopedia of Mystery and Detection* in an article on Annie titled "The Radio Murder Hour."

She listened attentively to ultra-Right philosophy and gave him prodding little pep talks when his fortunes were momentarily wiped away—in such diverse settings as palatial manor houses set in deep woods, metropolitan office buildings, and even a deserted cannibal island on which a mutineering crew had abandoned them. And when Oliver Warbucks was elsewhere making his empire grow, Annie enjoyed friendly chats with his two most trusted servants, Asp, the quiet Oriental killer, and the giant, scimitar-wielding, djinn-like Punjab. Punjab's devotion to the girl was obvious to all listeners; he was frequently to be found hovering close to her, rescuing her when danger approached, with a deep-throated: "We must come away, Little Princess."

Even the rustic towns to which Annie retreated were not without their dangers: crooked aldermen, grasping orphanage wardens, wicked landowners, proliferating arsonists, thieves of all descriptions, and as the program reached the war years, fifth columnists and foreign types whose names smacked of the Black Hand!

But all good things must end someday. In 1940, having apparently decided that kids were more interested in superheroes than little heroines, Ovaltine dropped Annie in favor of Captain Midnight. (Shirley Bell was included in the new show's cast.) The rest of the Chicago cast of *Orphan Annie* was let go, and the show moved to New York where Annie became the sidekick of an aviator named Captain Sparks (named after the show's new sponsor, Quaker Puffed Wheat Sparkies), but it was a dud and Annie went off the air for good in 1943.

No matter. By then, Annie had become a Hollywood star—twice.

The movie industry grew by leaps and bounds in the Thirties, and for twenty-five cents a ticket provided temporary relief from the Depression. The movie houses were jammed—an estimated 85 million people went to the movies every week—and the motion pictures became an insatiable devourer of any and all material that could be put in front of a camera.

In 1932, RKO Radio Pictures released *Little Orphan Annie*, which starred Bronx-born Mitzi Green in the title role. Gray cooperated fully in the film, for which David O. Selznick was executive producer and Max Steiner composed the music.

The plot was simple: Warbucks goes off on another of his business trips, and shortly afterward, Annie finds herself back in an orphanage. She becomes the object of the affection of a five-year-old boy named Mickey. When Mickey is adopted by a wealthy woman, Annie and Sandy go to visit him at his new home. Everything ends happily when Daddy comes home and throws a big Christmas party for everyone.

The movie was every bit as static as the plot implies. The most notable "performance" in it is Mitzi Green's adept impersonations of Groucho, Harpo, and Chico Marx. It opened on Christmas Eve,

1932. *Variety* found its plot "shallow," but without "a single objectionable moral"; the film, it said, "fits only as a good-will offering on the bottom of doubleheaders." The reviewer for the New York *Daily News* was "more than slightly disappointed" because the movie did not "do well by our Mr. Gray's Annie." The unnamed reviewer praised Miss Green's performance, but found her "too big and buxom" for the role.

In 1938, Paramount attempted its own motion pictures of the same title. It starred an actress named Ann Gilles. An anonymous reviewer at the time proclaimed it "stupid and thoroughly boresome," and seemed particularly put off by its "sugar-coated Pollyanna characterization."

It took another 40 years for Annie to make it to the silver screen again, and the third time around she finally got the kind of star treatment she deserved, in a very lavish production by Rastar Films and Columbia Pictures.

After *Little Orphan Annie* had become so popular, Gray liked to play around with it once in a while, poking good-natured fun at his own creation. Three years after Annie had gone to Hollywood for RKO, he sent her there himself in the panels of the comic strip.

Taking a break from a gang of Chinese tong killers out to skin her alive, Annie fell in with a dapper theatrical agent named Mr. Updown. He saw in her the perfect qualities for stardom—and a handsome commission for himself—because it just so happened that he knew a certain Hollywood producer who needed a good child performer right away. The movie mogul in question was Mr. Kolossal, embroiled in a contract dispute with the star of his new movie, a sniveling little harpy named Tootsie McSnoots, and the greedy parents who were holding up production so they could squeeze more money out of Kolossal.

Annie flew to Hollywood to be "discovered"—actually, to be the stand-in for Tootsie on long shots and dangerous stunts. Updown and Kolossal had it all planned, right down to the cheap wages they paid Annie, which seemed like a king's ransom to her but was a mere pittance compared with what Tootsie was getting.

Naturally, Annie was everything they hoped for and more—a real trouper who never flinched at the most hazardous stunts, including a parachute jump out of an airplane and a dive over a very high waterfall. But they made the mistake of boarding her with Janey Spangles, a struggling young starlet who quickly filled Annie in on all the dirt hidden behind the glitter of Hollywood.

In fact, would-be actors and actresses were streaming into Southern California by the busload at the time, all of them looking for the "big break" that would make them box-office idols. They were easily manipulated by the callous studio bosses, and many of them ended up the unhappy victims of types like Updown and Kolossal.

Annie was nobody's patsy, though. Once she knew how the game was played, she accepted it for what it was and had some good times with Janey before the sequence ended. She never became a movie star; Gray was smart enough never to let her get too successful.

Chapter 5

"WE'RE DOIN' *WAR* WORK"

America's long rehearsal for war ended at Pearl Harbor. Along with everyone else, the characters in *Little Orphan Annie* went marching off to war. Daddy, Punjab, and the Asp went in vaguely Allied uniforms, while Annie and Sandy fought on the home front. Even more than they had in the previous decade, Gray's themes for the comic strip during World War II came right from the front-page headlines. It resulted in mixed blessings: his inspiration of the national "Junior Commando" movement that enlisted thousands of children in the war effort was praised lavishly by public officials and the press, but an incident involving a feud with a local rationing-board official tarnished his image and made him appear a petty, vindictive man.

In 1940, it didn't take a prophet to see that the United States would inevitably be drawn into the war between the Axis and the Allies that had spread across Europe, Asia and Africa, or that the U.S. would go into it on the side of the Allies. But there was still a strong isolationist movement in America working to keep the country neutral. It had a national hero in its ranks, Charles Lindbergh, and a voice in the editorial columns of the New York *News* and the Chicago *Tribune*. The sister papers had been sniping away at Roosevelt and the New Deal from the beginning, so it was only consistent that they would object to Lend Lease and the overt preparations American military authorities were making for war.

"WE'RE DOIN' *WAR* WORK"

"Roosevelt's War, we think, is the correct name for the war in which we are engaging more intimately every day," the *News* said in an editorial published only a month before Pearl Harbor. A few days later, the *News* escalated its rhetoric: "We are now in the hands of military dictatorship, which apparently intends to proceed without consulting Congress beforehand as to any major move in his war."

But Daddy Warbucks was wide awake and on the job long before the first wave of Japanese planes approached Hawaii. He escaped from a concentration camp in an unnamed foreign country—readers were left very slightly to their own imaginations as to which one—where he had been imprisoned on one of his mysterious business trips. Back in America, Warbucks proceeded to live up to his name, converting his factories to full war production. In his own words, he was "back in harness, doing the job that must be done—the job I really know how to do." Gazing contentedly down on an assembly line filled with gleaming rows of airplanes, Daddy purred, "This is what I like best—producing, building. Motors, planes, tanks, ammunition. This is one job I know how to do."

The obvious relish with which Daddy was looking forward to direct involvement in the worldwide slaughter did not set well with everyone. Writing in the *American Mercury* ten months before Pearl Harbor, James Frank Vlamos lamented the stark realism that had overtaken so many of the comics.

"When headlines about dive-bombers and torpedoed transports become too much for your frayed nerves," Vlamos warned his readers, "don't for God's sake turn to the 'funnies' for relief. That colorful and carefree world in which you delighted in younger days—the world of slapstick and innocent jokes, of grotesque but lovable creatures—has all but disappeared. . . . The carefree and jolly world of the comics has turned brutal, violent and fake-scientific."

He cited a recent episode of *Little Orphan Annie* that had begun as a case of small-time political corruption but had blossomed into a sinister tale of international intrigue, featuring that no-good spy and nemesis of America, the notorious "Axel."

"Once upon a time Little Orphan Annie showed her dexterity by getting out of mild small-town scrapes, foiling pinchpenny mortgage holders and neighborhood hoodlums," Vlamos wrote. "Skipping gory details, suffice it that on Annie's frail shoulders now rests the fate of our nation. She can be depended on to see the thing through whatever the cost in villainous blood. . . . So don't look for escape in the current 'funnies.' Stick to the saner world of war and horror on the front pages."

47

Vlamos was obviously not a longtime reader of *Little Orphan Annie*, or he would have known that there hadn't been anything "funny" about it for years.

Six months after the United States entered the war, Daddy returned from yet another of his clandestine journeys, dressed in the uniform of a three-star general.

"Why not?" he explained to Annie. "I've had considerable experience as a soldier. A soldier of fortune, mostly. Fighting to win millions for myself, it's true. But I *did* win. I know the men of the jungle, and the men of the jungle know me. And *this* time we're fighting for something no money can buy."

"But that uniform, Daddy. I don't see 'U.S.' on it at all," Annie observed.

"Oh, well, you see, Annie, I got in a little ahead of schedule. After all, we're out to lick the same gang." In all situations, Daddy did things only on his own terms.

Faster than you could say "Heil Hitler," Warbucks revealed the reason for his return. Another eccentric inventor, this one named Mr. Zane, had developed a very powerful explosive device that would, Daddy explained to Annie, revolutionize modern warfare. It was an intriguing foreshadowing by Gray of the atomic bomb that would make its terrible debut more than three years later. Daddy's mission was to deliver Zane's secret formula to "the right people." With a big hug for Annie and the bravado of a departing warrior, he drove off with Punjab and the Asp—who were also in uniform—and predicted that "a week from today we'll be in contact with the enemy."

They were barely out of sight when Annie acquired a new chum, a pudgy teenage boy named Panda. The two of them stumbled onto a Nazi submarine hidden in a nearby cove. Snaring a huge mine with their rowboat, Annie and Panda towed it to the submarine, which blew up. The handful of survivors were then sent to kingdom come when Panda inadvertently tripped a wire linked to a booby trap. Incredibly, a real German U-boat was detected and sunk off the Atlantic coast some months later.

Without missing a beat, Gray then launched Annie on the crusade that became her—and his—first contribution to the war effort: the Junior Commandos.

Annie and a schoolmate, Loretta, came into some chiding from the other girls in town because they always seemed to be too busy to play. "Loretta an' I have somethin' lots more important than playin'," Annie replied. "We're doin' *war* work. It's *our* war, just as much—or maybe more—than anybody else's. We're *givin'* all we can to help those who are *givin'* ever'thing for us!"

The Junior Commando movement was formalized on a Sunday color page. Gray, never subtle when a great cause was concerned, made it perfectly clear that the Commandos would be a very starched outfit. Annie—*Colonel* Annie, as she came to call herself—kept a ledger with the name of every person in town written in it.

"Now, next to th' name o' everyone who helped by givin' old iron or paper or 'luminum, we make a *blue* mark," she explained to a subordinate. "Those who hire Junior Commandos to run errands so we can use th' money to buy war stamps, get a *red* mark." And what about those who don't do anything? "If they won't even *try* to help when our country needs th' help o' everyone? Why, that's easy—for them we use a *yellow* mark!"

Thus began one of the most successful domestic operations of the war. The Junior Commando movement sent thousands of youngsters scrambling through junkpiles and knocking on doors to round up newspapers, scrap metal, old tires, kitchen grease—all the raw materials needed to feed the factories that were manufacturing war products.

Within a month after Annie lectured her young pals about doing their bit, Junior Commando chapters were being organized all across the country, to the delight of parents, press, and war-production officials. Gray, who had taken it on the chin plenty of times during his scraps with the New Dealers, for once could bask in the warm glow of praise from every quarter.

"Some of the fat, shiny salvos soon to serenade Schickelgruber and Co. are sure to be earmarked, 'With love and kisses from the Junior Commandos, U.S.A.'" the Tribune syndicate crowed in a press-released headline "Salvos from Salvage for Dictators." It detailed the formation of one Junior Commando group in Erie, Pennsylvania:

"Rank in the Commandos is determined by how much scrap each member brings in. The officers of this particular Erie group now boast a 12-year-old captain, an 11-year-old lieutenant and a 10-year-old sergeant. Collections are made each morning from 10 to 12 o'clock. These Erie Commandos each have a block or two to cover and visit each house once a week. Sometimes in their salvage quest they are invited to have milk and cookies. Just how serious Young America is taking this adult war is indicated by the many letters received by Harold Gray, Annie's creator. All of them request enlistment in the Junior Commandos. We quote the young captain from Erie: 'This is our war, too, and we want to give all we can to help the soldiers who are giving all they have.'"

The Rochester, New York, *Democrat and Chronicle* said the Junior Commando movement "strikes the fancy of boys and girls who want to help win the war. . . . These kids are accomplishing things that adults have failed in.

"Boys and girls of the Junior Commandos work with two motives," the article continued, "they want to help, and they want to earn another stripe on their arm chevrons. All awards are made on a merit basis. When an applicant joins, his questionnaire must be signed by a parent and the commanding officer of the unit he joins. If he is forming a new unit, only the parent need sign. A reviewing board meets weekly to pass on applications. If they are accepted, credential cards are issued. Advances in rank are based upon reports of unit commanding officers or the further recommendation of parents. Arm chevrons with one stripe denoting the rank of second lieutenant are issued when earned. Two stripes are for first lieutenant, three for captain and three stripes and a star for the commanding officer of a company of four units."

In other words, the biggest difference between a kid signing up for the Junior Commandos and his or her older brother going to boot camp might have been getting inoculated.

Shortly after the Junior Commandos were launched, an article in *Editor & Publisher* reported that both Gray and the Tribune syndicate were "pleasantly surprised because what was viewed as nothing more than a simple change in continuity has developed into one of the best promotions ever to come out of the syndicate.

"This is no willy-nilly affair offering bright badges and peashooters," *E & P* declared. "It's the real thing, and it's worth your life to try to tell a 'Commando' that it isn't. They've already turned over tons of scrap collected in their spare time and they're still going strong."

By the fall of 1942, the editor of the Boston *Herald Traveler* reported that there were "close to 20,000 Junior Commandos enrolled and filed under localities throughout Metropolitan Boston." He was careful, however, to note that the paper "wished to avoid the suspicion that it was solely an advertising stunt in the beginning, and wanted to definitely establish that it was a part of the great war movement."

In March 1943, *Coronet* magazine published a four-color poster of Annie in her Junior Commando uniform, and pronounced her "more of a heroine than Joan of Arc, more tragic and appealing than Helen of Troy, and far more real than the current glamour girl to 50,000 people of assorted sizes and shapes and of all ages." "The Junior Commando movement," *Coronet* said, "marked the change from a comic strip to a cosmic strip. . . . When Annie launched the Junior Commando movement, she did the children of the nation a tremendous favor—and she did the nation a favor as well."

That was rare praise for a man whose attacks on the social programs of Roosevelt had made him a pariah in liberal circles. Gray continued Annie's Junior Commando activities throughout the war, and gave the Commandos the satisfaction of smashing a Nazi spy ring.

But just as surely as he never let Annie find that happy ending she always dreamed of, neither did Gray have a chance to rest on his laurels for very long. Controversy and criticism seemed to permanently flank his drawing board.

Packed off by Daddy to the fictional small town of Gooneyville, Annie went to live with a middle-aged couple named Spike and Sally Spangle. She hadn't been in town very long when she caused great embarrassment both to Gray and to the Tribune syndicate. It was an incident that might have been labeled the "Fred Flask Flap." It began, as usual, with Gray baiting a government bear.

The war had brought rationing of fuel, food, and other basic commodities, which was a great inconvenience to individual citizens. Local boards (part of the federal Office of Price Administration) were established in each community to allocate scarce items, in an attempt to insure not only maximum efficiency but also fair treatment for everyone. Like the draft board that decided who should go off to fight, the ration boards were made up of ordinary citizens guided by their own common sense and a set of regulations from Washington. Predictably, some of the thousands of people appointed to these boards used the power at their disposal to feather their own nests. And just as predictably, some of the citizens who were forced to live with the dicta set down by the boards were unhappy. One of them was Harold Gray, of Westport, Connecticut.

Jurisdiction for the area where he lived belonged to the ration board operating out of the neighboring town of Fairfield. The Chairman of that board was named Robert C. Flack. Taking the position that it was necessary for him to travel around so he could gather material for *Little Orphan Annie*, Gray applied to the board for extra gas coupons, which would have entitled him to buy as much automobile fuel as someone whose activities were deemed vital to the war effort. But the ration board didn't think someone who listed his occupation as "cartoonist-artist" was an important cog in the machinery of victory; Gray's application was denied, and that meant the former free-wheeling spirit would be limited to a few local trips each week.

Gray exercised his right to a hearing before the full board, which in the end voted to sustain the original denial. Gray was enraged, and exchanged heated words with Flack. But to no avail—he was grounded. Smoldering, he returned to his drawing board.

Some time later, in the panels of *Little Orphan Annie*, Uncle Spike and Aunt Sally explain to Annie that they'd sold their car because they couldn't buy gas for it. Seemed their gas coupons had been taken away entirely by the head of Gooneyville's ration board when it was discovered that Aunt Sally had driven an elderly neighbor to the hospital to visit a sick relative. This good deed was determined to have been a frivolous waste of vital gasoline by the head of the Gooneyville ration board, "Fred Flask."

"Gee whiz! That seemed like an awful mean trick," Annie exclaimed.

"Oh, he says he doesn't make the rules," Uncle Spike replied. "Hmm—it takes all kinds to win a war, I guess."

Had he left it at that, Gray might have kept intact the laurels he'd won for the Junior Commandos. But there was nothing moderate about his temperament, and once his fuse was lit, it was not easily extinguished. For three more days, including a full page on Sunday, "Fred Flask" was raked over the coals in the hundreds of newspapers that ran *Little Orphan Annie*.

"Hey look! Whose swell sports car is that goin' by?" Annie asked as she looked out the Spangles' front window.

"Oh, that's Mr. Flask," Aunt Sally said. "He's on official business, of course. He *has* to drive."

"I'll bet he hates that!" Annie remarked. "I thought his car was a sedan."

"Oh, the sedan belongs to *Mrs*. Flask," Sally answered. "She needs it for shopping and other essential activities." That day's strip was headlined "Double Standard." The following day's installment bore the headline "Oh, Happy Coincidence," and featured this exchange:

"*Two* cars? Why, the Flasks have *three*—their son has to get to and from school," Uncle Spike informed Annie.

"He goes to the academy over at Burpley," Aunt Sally chimed in. "No bus at the right time."

"So he drives back and forth each day, eh?" Annie remarked. "Fifty miles. But o' course, it's *essential*."

"Seems it is, with his father interpreting the rules," Uncle Spike agreed.

"Fred Flask has to do an awful *lot* o' driving," Annie persisted. "Gone all day yesterday."

"Oh, he went to Motleyville to check on a plant," Uncle Spike explained. "Seems their employees have been driving too much. He just *happened* to be there on the day of his cousin's wedding over there."

Over the course of the next few days, Uncle Spike went on to complain about government forms "to be filled out in triplicate," how lousy business was under price controls, and how poorly the local salvage drive was going because the head of it, the mayor's wife, was a "public nuisance." On and on it went, day after day of Uncle Spike and Aunt Sally bellyaching about this, that, and the other thing—to the point it was a wonder Gray wasn't locked up himself for undermining public morale.

The locals jumped all over him for the "Fred Flask" bit. A front-page article in the weekly Fairfield *News* asked, "Is Orphan Annie Hitting Below Belt by Co-incidence?"

"The long arm of coincidence this week served to pair Harold Gray's comic strip character Orphan Annie and Robert C. Flack, chairman of the local ration board," was the lead paragraph of the story, which observed that if one letter is changed in the name of Gray's character Flask, "the name becomes 'Flack,' corresponding to the name of the head of Fairfield's ration board. But Mr. Gray's 'Mr. Flask' is apparently a despicable character, and according to those more familiar with the evolutions of comic strips, Annie will shortly have a hand in exposing the nefarious and personal favor-tinged doings of this Mr. Flask.

"Fairfield's Mr. Flack, on the other hand, has headed a board which since its origination has had a reputation as easily the best run board in this part of the country. This statement has been made by Chester Bowles who is now national OPA administrator."

The weekly's article went on to point out that ration-board heads did not possess the power to single-handedly take away a citizen's ration book. And it declared that "both Mr. and Mrs. Flack are giving six days a week, gratis, to the Town of Fairfield as volunteer workers in the war effort. There has never been the slightest suspicion that Mr. and Mrs. Flack have usurped favors for themselves. In fact, they have denied themselves more than any other rationed individual in town."

Notoriety has its price. Were it not for the fact that *Little Orphan Annie* was so widely distributed, or the fact that ration boards existed in every American community, or the fact that Gray's past attacks had made him a host of enemies who itched for revenge, the Flask/Flack fiasco might have been ignored.

It was not. The week after the "Fred Flask" strips appeared, the staunchly pro-Roosevelt Louisville *Courier-Journal* yanked *Little Orphan Annie* out of its daily comics page (although it continued to print the Sunday installment). For once, a flood of letters and telephone calls from the paper's readers complaining about the absence of the strip did not get it restored immediately.

"*Little Orphan Annie* was dropped because its sponsors, a syndicate controlled by the New York *Daily News* and the Chicago *Tribune*, had turned it into a vehicle of propaganda against gasoline rationing," the *Courier-Journal*'s editors wrote to their readers. "The *Courier-Journal*, as readers of this letter column, of our columnists and of our reports of controversial news and speeches know, does not mind presenting opinions contrary to our own. Nevertheless, we have to insist that opinion of whatever kind be duly labeled as such and not smuggled into comic strips in the guise of entertainment."

But another paper, the *Republican-American* in Waterbury, Connecticut, saw ration boards "squirming" over the Fred Flask episode, and it warned against possible attempts by federal ration officials to censor the press.

Editor & Publisher dutifully reported the Tribune Syndicate's denial of allegations that the content of *Little Orphan Annie* was being dictated by either Patterson or McCormack. "It was Gray's own idea," a syndicate spokesman said. "In fact, when we first saw the continuity we were under the impression that it would run only a few days. So we let it go through. When we saw that it was running longer than expected and that the theme was strongly on the propaganda side, we informed our clients that we were canceling the rest of the strips and substituting new ones for them."

Later, when Flack theatened to sue the syndicate and Gray for libel, a statement was published in the *Daily News*: "We have been informed by Mr. Robert C. Flack, chairman of the local rationing board of Fairfield, Conn., that the portrayal of the character, Fred Flask, was generally understood by people in his community and by many people elsewhere in Connecticut as having reference to him. The News Syndicate Co. is glad to make it perfectly clear that it did not intend, directly or indirectly, to refer to Mr. Flack or any other living person. It published the strip in good faith, in the belief that the characters, including the character Fred Flask, were entirely fictitious. The News Syndicate Co. sincerely regrets any damage or embarrassment that may have been caused Mr. Flack."

Gray, however, was not in the least contrite. He told *E & P* that the whole episode was "a tempest in a teapot."

"I took anything I have used out of the daily newspapers. I made nothing up out of my head," he said. "I can't for the life of me see how any citizen can live in a community and not be affected by the

OPA, especially as regards gasoline rationing. The OPA's state of obfuscation laid them open to a little kidding, which is all I did. Which is all I intended to do. However, the syndicate has asked me to drop the continuity and I have complied. I rather suspect the cartoons struck home in what they were showing or they would have been ignored."

As for the similarity between the names Flask and Flack, Gray had an energetic but not very convincing explanation: "We have a standing rule in the business which calls for us to use inanimate objects as subjects for our names. The name 'Flask' came to me as I was thinking of snoopers. Snoopers brought to mind Prohibition. And the next logical thought was the hip flask. That's how I arrived at that name. I'm sorry if it has inconvenienced the OPA gentleman. I assure you it was pure coincidence."

But Gray had "inconvenienced" more than one OPA official. He received many letters from ration-board members across the country. One of them, from a board member in a small Michigan community, enlightened him about what it felt like on the other side of the fence:

"The job as you well know is a most thankless one—undoubtedly the dirtiest public service one can be called upon to render. Screwy regulations are very difficult to explain to 'cranks,' and we are constantly and perpetually damned for our decisions. The average person receives the decision as a personal matter—feels that he has been discriminated against, and is prone to consider every ration board member as an enemy. While there may be a precious few ration board members in the 5,000 local boards who are not above personal favoritism, the 4,999 who *are* doing their level best to give their fellow citizens a square deal will be (or at least are temporarily) placed under a shadow of doubt. Nope, I don't think it's right! We have enough stuff thrown in our face now."

Gray was not without supporters, though. "Congratulations to Annie," wrote a woman from Unionville, Connecticut. "Keep up the good work. You have put your finger on a sore spot. There is proof of what you say to be seen all around us. While some of us deny ourselves conscientiously, the rest go on their merry way as if there was no war."

Fred Flask didn't bother the editorial writers at the Bridgeport *Herald* nearly so much as Uncle Spike and Aunt Sally, "who spend 100% of their time griping about rationing and price control." The *Herald*, published just a few miles from Gray's home, remarked that Annie's experiences with the Spangles in Gooneyville "sound like pages from the diary of a die-hard Republican of the America First persuasion.

"Whatever became of Annie's knack for spreading sweetness and light around this dark world—for teaching her elders the lesson of harmony, patience and courage?" the *Herald* asked. "The kid seems to have lost her touch."

Life went on in Gooneyville, where Annie formed a chapter of the Junior Commandos, and Spike Spangle was punished for all his carping by going broke. Gray, however, was utterly unrepentant. A few punches thrown his way seemed to bring out the college boxer in him. When he put on the gloves, it was usually with a pen in his hand. But sometimes he used a typewriter.

Gray took to the keyboard from time to time and replied directly—and usually at great length—to the letters he received that stirred up his inner juices. In the midst of the Flask controversy, he had received a letter from then-Congresswoman Claire Booth Luce (wife of *Time* publisher Henry Luce), who had been elected from Gray's home district in 1943. Mrs. Luce, a fellow Republican, had expressed her sympathies to him for all the knocks he had taken. His long, typewritten reply to her revealed his motives for drawing *Little Orphan Annie* the way he did:

It makes it a little rough sometimes, to avoid all politics, since Annie is supposed to be a part of her community. And what community is without politics? Anyone who regards comics today as "funnies" is living twenty or thirty years in the past. The successful comics today are stories. No story is worth printing unless it carries some idea. And any idea is the basis for disagreement and hence is controversial. Of course only a sucker would intentionally make people mad in a strip he wished to circulate widely. But for many years I have tried as best I can to know the changing thoughts of folks, not only here, but along the West Coast, in Texas and across the South and back and forth all over this country and Canada. I believe the fundamentals of honesty, hard work, and thrift are still held dearly by the vast majority of Americans, in spite of wisecracks to the contrary, and in spite of passing waves of hysteria. Annie sticks to those basic ideals, hence she is a lousy Fascist, according to some vocal subscribers who apparently can read the pictures, though they can't write too well.

My contention is that since strips tell a story of the current scene, and since many columnists whose stuff is heavily weighted one way or the other enjoy vast circulation, why wouldn't a strip such as Annie also be very popular if allowed to really tell the American story? Annie will never get the green light. With the standing rule against "comment" in any strip she'd be excommunicated if she tried it. But there is a tremendous opening in such a venture for the one who breaks ground and first enters that forbidden field. I'd like to be that guy. A strip that is properly handled has tremendous power. As a political weapon it must be handled much as Swift handled the British problem of his day in *Gulliver's Travels*.

Lest you get the impression that I am a crusader, may I tell you that I decidedly despise bleeding hearts and professional reformers. But I still think a properly handled political strip would go like a prairie fire and be even hotter.

Maybe Gray didn't realize at the time that he had already reached that goal. Or maybe he was thinking of the more literal, undisguised political comic strip that would not come to pass until nearly three decades later, when Garry Trudeau's *Doonesbury* became the Watergate chronicles. Whatever he was thinking at the time, he still held a spleen full of venom for Franklin Roosevelt. His closing line in the letter to Mrs. Luce read: "Please give my regards to our RULER when you see him."

Another glimpse of his raw thinking had come out of Gray's typewriter a year earlier. It had been dispatched to the publisher of a newspaper in Alabama, who had objected to the presence in Annie's Junior Commando unit of a youngster named George. George had been promoted to sergeant by virtue of being a highly productive member of the group. George was black. The Alabama publisher had sent a letter to Gray noting that while he had knowledge of "only two or three subscribers who stated that they had read Orphan Annie for the last time because of mixing a Negro character in with the white children," he felt compelled to suggest that in future Gray give "careful thought and due consideration to the problems of the South on this issue.

"Right or wrong," the publisher went on, "it is a most inopportune time to unnecessarily raise any issue which would result in controversy and conflict between the races. At least, it should be deferred until it will in no way interfere with our war effort. I sincerely hope that you can eliminate the use of the Negro boy character in the future."

Gray's single-page reply was more apologetic than anything else. It left the impression that equality of the races was not among the causes he felt compelled to champion.

The use of the character George, he wrote, was "more tactical than tactful. God knows I'm no reformer. I am fully as strongly in favor of the South, or any other section of the country handling its own problems. I am no relation to Mrs. Roosevelt [an early and ardent proponent of civil rights] either, nor do I subscribe in any way to the text that the color line should be broken down."

Gray went on to explain that Annie's continuing ·popularity depended on "her ability to build and hold friendships with all classes," and that she "fraternizes with Jews, Chinese, East Indians, tramps, gangsters of the golden-hearted and rough exterior type, even with the Clergy." He noted that New York was "the largest colored city in the world," and that other large Northern cities where Annie's circulation numbers ran very high "all have large dark towns." As a result of that, the inclusion of George in the Junior Commandos was "merely a casual gesture toward a very large block of readers."

That block of readers sent many letters to Gray thanking him for including a black character in his strip—letters that probably wouldn't have been written if they'd known he was whining about a numbers game to an Alabama publisher. Black readers expressed their gratitude that their children had been given a visible and positive sign that mainstream American society had a place for them, too. But if Gray replied to any of those letters, the copies he customarily made are missing from his papers.

In the summer of 1944, the Democratic Party nominated Roosevelt for an unprecedented fourth term as President. It was more than a "Republican right down to his toenails" could stand. Clearly, the world was not big enough for both Franklin Roosevelt and Oliver Warbucks. Gray killed off Warbucks.

The word "dramatic" doesn't do proper justice to the pathos-laden sequence that went on for a solid month as Daddy, in the throes of a "fever" he'd contracted while fighting in the jungle, gradually slipped deeper and deeper into the grave. Not a single drop of maudlin sentiment was held back: Gray gave his alter ego a funeral befitting Julius Caesar, George Washington, and Abraham Lincoln, all rolled into one.

Even before he actually kicked the bucket, a woman who had been a friend and confidante, and was now his nurse, was walking around delivering eulogies for Warbucks to anyone who would listen: "He gave his plants . . . his business . . . his fortune! Every dime for what he believed in! For a way of life we *all* believe in . . . or *most* of us do!"

With those words ringing in her ears, Annie was determined to be strong in the face of this catastrophe: "Daddy's goin' to die, but I won't cry. Not *yet* anyway. N-n-not yet . . ."

The headlines on the strips that week were: "The Lamp Is Low,"

"WE'RE DOIN' *WAR* WORK"

"Mr. Death," "When You've Got To Go," and "Here's Where He Gets Off." Could there have been a dry eye in the house as Daddy imparted his final wisdoms to little Annie?

"Death isn't bad," he said cheerfully, his fever-wracked body wrapped in blankets. "He comes to all of us, Annie. I've found he's really not a bad chap at all—for the brave. Only cowards *fear* death. I've had a good life. I've been successful, but I'm not ashamed of that. I've been honest and, I think, fairly decent. I've lived my life according to my time and generation. Probably it's *time* for me to go!"

A tearful Annie helped him up onto the soapbox for one last harangue. "What do you mean, it's *time* for you to go?" she asked.

"I've been what's called a capitalist. Some have called me 'dirty capitalist.' But I've merely used the imagination and common sense and energy that kind providence gave me. It made me wealthy . . . powerful . . . hated by some, admired by others. But now? Well, Annie, times have changed and I'm old and tired. I guess it's time to go!"

"But you were always so kind and good and generous!" Annie protested.

"Maybe I could *afford* to be generous," Warbucks replied. "I never did enjoy being a failure, I'm happy to say."

Then, if anyone could still read through their sopping handkerchiefs, came the final embrace.

"You, Annie, will go on to a new day!" Daddy said by way of benediction. "May it be a bright and happy day—for you and for all of your hopeful, happy companions! Good luck, Annie . . . my darling!"

"Oh, Daddy!" she sobbed, hugging him. "I'll love you for ever and ever!"

Mercifully, Gray spared his audience the spectacle of Daddy's corpse being lowered in the cold, cold ground. Perhaps he was reserving the right to revive him someday. The last rites for the martyr of capitalism concluded with Annie's lonely vigil on a starlit night, with Sandy at her side.

"It . . . it's really happened. Daddy . . . gone! For keeps!" On her knees, her hands clasped in prayer, she turned her face heavenward. "Oh, Daddy! Wherever you are . . . I'll *never* forget you. And I'll go on loving you for ever and ever!"

If there was a heart anywhere so hard that it wasn't reduced to a blubbering mass after *that* send-off, it went unnoticed among the sorrowing throng that had just witnessed Harold Gray's funeral service for himself.

Reaction to the passing of Warbucks was generally—but not entirely—unfavorable. A postcard from West Virginia arrived in Gray's mail: "Well, you've killed Daddy Warbucks. You can bring him back to life again. I and the American public want it this way, I'm sure. Maybe Punjab could do it with his East Indian magic. Please get him back in sooner or later."

But a New York City man said he was happy to see Warbucks out of the way, and hoped it would be only the beginning of the complete genocide of *Little Orphan Annie* characters: "Congratulations to Harold Gray for bumping off that loathsome character Daddy Warbucks. Please instruct him to get rid of Orphan Annie some time in the near future in the most violent manner possible, and bring an end to years of wasted newsprint. She is the most awful character ever, with her eternal prying, snooping, preaching and stale philosophy. I am quite sure that I am not the only one who feels that her time is long overdue."

The manager of an insurance office in Columbus, Ohio, viewed Daddy's demise in a practical vein. He pointed out the regrettable shortsightedness of Warbucks in not carrying a hefty amount of life insurance to provide for Annie after he was gone, and said the consensus among the salesmen on his staff was that Gray "would have made a great Life Insurance man!"

A reader in Pennsylvania sent an ornate sympathy card, and conservative publisher William Loeb, a dedicated fan of Daddy Warbucks, sent his personal condolences.

One might have imagined that *Little Orphan Annie* could have ended right there. Or, its essential structure gone, it might have moved off in another direction. Nope. Gray had just begun to punish America for its persecution and execution of Warbucks and his breed of capitalist. Annie was about to be put through the most harrowing ordeal to date, and in the process Gray nearly broke his readers' hearts. By the time Election Day ("Coronation Day," he might have termed it) rolled around, things had gotten as bad for Annie as they ever would.

Daddy's bones were hardly chilled when the doorbell rang and standing outside was "Mrs. J. Bleating-Hart," the local child-welfare official who was the supreme caricature of the social worker with a soul of coal dust. To make her especially hateful, Gray assigned her a phony Boston Brahmin accent.

The fat, bespectacled Mrs. Bleating-Hart arranged for Annie to be placed in an orphans' home. In short order, though, she took her into her own household, ostensibly as an act of charity—shades of the first

Mrs. Warbucks!—though it soon became clear that Mrs. B-H had decided that here was a new servant.

Outfitted in a maid's uniform, doing a maid's chores from dawn to dusk, Annie was enrolled in the local school but had no time to do her homework. Her teacher, a kind young woman named Mrs. Ivy, was aware of how Annie was being treated at home, but could do nothing about it because Mrs. Bleating-Hart happened to be the head of the local school board.

The outrages piled up faster than Warbucks' millions: Mrs. Bleating-Hart ordered Sandy put to sleep—but the dogcatcher, Sam Setter, saved him; a schoolmate's mother bought Annie a new dress to replace the tattered one Mrs. B-H had picked up at a rummage sale, but the old goat made Annie give it back; Annie even tried to sass her way back to the orphanage, but the crafty old battlewagon caught on and wouldn't fall for it. To cap it all, Mrs. Bleating-Hart's no-good, deadbeat son Melvin came home after being expelled from private school and took it upon himself to make each day more miserable for Annie than the last.

By the time Christmas Day rolled around, Annie was wondering if she'd ever see a sunny day again; her Christmas present from Mrs. Bleating-Hart was an old alarm clock—so she'd be sure to wake up early enough each morning to clean the house from top to bottom before going to school. By then, there was a mountain of letters piled up on Gray's desk, all of them pleading for him to have mercy on the poor little girl.

The U.S. Secretary of Commerce, Jesse Jones, was moved to write a terse message on official stationery: "She's too tough. Can't wait much longer."

A poignant handwritten note signed "Orphan Dorothy" came from New Hyde Park, Long Island: "Please get Orphan Annie out of Mrs. Bleating-Hart's clutches real soon," she begged. "You are breaking my heart. Having been placed in one of those so-called opportunity homes after losing one of my parents, I had about the same experiences, yes, some worse than Orphan Annie's. Sad to say there are plenty of Mrs. Bleating-Hart's sort, who being too lazy to do their own work offer out of the kindness of their big hearts an opportunity home to some orphan, an opportunity for whom, and what?"

A gentleman in Fort Arthur, Texas, sent a carefully typed letter: "You are going to have to do something about Mrs. Bleedingheart (*sic*) and stop her oppression of Orphan Annie pretty soon, or you will have all of us so upset that we are going to be unable to carry on our normal daily activities. Our maid came in to the breakfast table the other morning, laid the paper down and said: 'That Mrs. Bleedingheart is making me sick. I can't eat thinking how shameful she is treating Orphan Annie.' Our whole family feels the same way about it, and thinks it is about time Mrs. Bleedingheart meets with her comeuppance. Please do something about it quick!''

Gray did do something about it—he bumped off Mrs. Bleating-Hart, and then framed Annie for her murder. All alone, with an incompetent lawyer as her defender, she faced the prosecution in a sequence that had trial lawyers shrieking with indignation from one end of the continent to the other.

"In no court in the land could lawyer, judge and jury combine in such a perversion of justice to railroad a child to conviction," wrote an attorney in Pittsburgh. "You might as well reflect on the medical profession by depicting a little child as seriously ill and the attending physician purposely permitting her to suffer or die by deliberately refusing to apply appropriate medical treatment. . . . Your portrayal of the trial of Annie for murder has done incalculable harm, particularly among the young, to destroy any confidence in the administration of justice. If you care to make amends, you might have an Appellate Court reverse the conviction, impeach the Judge, disbar Lawyer Thimble and disqualify the members of the Jury from ever again serving as jurors."

The Mansfield, Ohio, *News-Journal*, however, made light of an indignant letter sent to Gray by the Attorney General of the State of California accusing Gray of "seriously attacking the tradition of the American bench and bar."

"It is unlikely that honest and capable judges and lawyers will get into disrepute as a result of the possibly slightly exaggerated portrayal being indulged in by the creator of *Orphan Annie* characters," the paper said in an editorial. "We're still betting that Annie's detractors will come to no good end."

Annie was indeed cleared of the charges against her in the end, just as Daddy Warbucks had been cleared of the accusations against him during the time of Samuel Insull. But that was nothing compared to one of the biggest events of 1945. Toward the end of the summer, Oliver Warbucks was brought back from the dead.

He was resurrected in true Gray style, spouting the doctrine of good old capitalism under headlines on the strip that said "Half A Loaf, But No Loafer," "America First," and "His Creed." It seemed that Daddy had been just playing dead before, in order to foil his enemies and accomplish "a very special secret job."

What had made it possible was the death, in April 1945, of

Roosevelt. In a bold victory chant that is shocking to this day, War-bucks tap-danced on FDR's grave.

"You were sayin' that maybe it was the *climate* here, that made you sick before?" a very relieved Annie remarked.

"It could have been, I sure *was* sick," a self-satisfied Warbucks replied, puffing healthily on his cigar and gazing serenely out the window.

"But then, won't the climate make you sick again, now that you're back?" she persisted.

"Hm-m-m . . . I don't think so, Annie. I feel fine, so far," he said, casually examining his cigar ash. "Somehow I feel that the *climate* here has *changed* since I went away. We'll see."

"Gee! They said some awful nasty things 'bout you, Daddy, when they thought you were dead."

"Ha-ha!" Daddy cackled gleefully. "I got quite a kick reading my obituaries! I guess it was fashionable to sneer at 'big incomes.' They failed to mention that most of those big incomes go to pay every-body's bills, and make the load lighter for everyone else. I believe that the more a man makes honestly, the more he helps this country, and everybody in it. What I think we need is a lot *more* million-a-year men! Mighty little *they* can *keep* anyway."

That was about as succinct a modern-day expression of Calvinism as has been written in the last two centuries. Thus revived was the unrepentant, unreconstructed, unabashed icon of capitalism. The war was over. Roosevelt was dead. America was back in business. And so was Oliver Warbucks, professional billionaire.

Chapter 6

"WHAT A GIRL!"

The postwar years may have been dull in some quarters, but not in the panels of *Little Orphan Annie*. With FDR dead and the enemies of freedom defeated, Gray went hunting for other targets. He found plenty. Some of them shot back.

Annie and her friends struggled unsuccessfully to keep The Bomb out of the hands of the International Communist Conspiracy, and blood flowed through the strip by the barrelful as they tussled with the tyranny of organized labor, teenage hoodlums, Chinese Reds, Russian Reds, American Reds, plus the familiar assortment of crooked cops and politicians, thugs, gangsters, loafers, and other undesirables. In the process, Gray became the target of counterassaults from union leaders, clergymen, liberals, and a fair number of newspaper and magazine editors.

The most ordinary event in *Little Orphan Annie* could provoke a hue and cry. In 1947, Annie got a job delivering groceries. That seemed an innocuous enough development. But Annie was not your ordinary delivery girl. When a customer suggested that she might have more fun out playing with other kids, she launched into a long-winded speech that boiled down to the opinion that if all youngsters were put to work they wouldn't have time to get into trouble.

That brought a predictable response from the labor movement. "We have to confess that either we are losing our sense of humor or that Little Orphan has ceased to be very funny," wrote a columnist for a machinists' association. "A few years back, the Little Orphan used to campaign against trade unions. More recently Annie has been hard at work showing us how silly are all the laws against child labor. Now we know that newspaper publishers never have liked child labor laws for fear that they would stop kids peddling papers. We don't think peddling papers hurts anyone. It didn't hurt us. But that's no reason to send kids back into the textile mills and canneries when they should be in school."

Another labor newspaper, the *Union Times*, editorialized that Annie's speechmaking was a "naked call for unrestrained child labor.

"The insidious nature of Gray's artful advocacy of the child labor cause through the medium of an innocent (and therefore most effective) comic strip character, with many millions of readers, is threatening," the paper continued. "After a frightful war was fought to prove it, we now recognize that special training and education are musts for our children, as they are the leaders of tomorrow. Any suggestion that they be detoured into the bowels of industry or the business world is a menace to the very system and traditional progress that America represents."

That kind of talk got Gray's blood boiling. He let fly during an interview with the Chicago *Tribune* Sunday magazine.

"A little work never hurt any kid," he fumed. "Lord's sake, I was running a four-horse team in a field when I was nine years old. One of the reasons we have so much juvenile delinquency these days is that kids are forced by law to loaf around on street corners and get into trouble. Annie wanted to work and I saw no harm in letting her deliver packages to earn a little spending money."

That outburst seemed to come from a protective father rather than a cartoonist whose creation existed only on paper and ink—a fact that was not lost on the *Tribune* interviewer, who observed that Gray "talks about her as if she were a regular member of the family. He always says, 'Annie did thus and so'—never 'I had her do it' or 'I drew her doing thus and so.' In his enthusiasm for her, he becomes totally unconscious of the fact that she is a figment of his own imagination, a funny-paper puppet who moves only when he pulls the strings. . . . So serious is he, so realistic in discussing her ambitions and escapades, that one suddenly has an uncannily vivid impression of her actual presence, as if the wide-eyed little moppet had just entered the room. This undoubtedly is the secret of Annie's success as a comic strip. She is fashioned from a fond father's dreams, with all the tenderness and care and faith and ideals any man would have for his child."

In a private counterpoint to that paternal ode, Gray wrote these words on the inside back cover of his diary book for 1946: "Writer never gets story told—So many ideas—Mind like dusty, cluttered attic. Full of stuff that will never bring him a cent. Should clean it out and start an antique shop." Written below, apparently as an afterthought, was: "Orphans should be illegal."

Taking a chunk out of Harold Gray's hide got to be a popular sport in the postwar years. Many of the attacks came from predictable sources, but some did not. At one point, he was simultaneously accused of being a right-wing warmonger and a Communist subversive.

The former charge appeared in a London newspaper column written by a man who used the pseudonym "Cassandra." He found fault with a *Little Orphan Annie* sequence in which Daddy Warbucks retrieved one of his engineers from the clutches of the Chinese Reds by obliterating a main government office building. ("I never bluff," Daddy remarked calmly.) Cassandra saw in that attitude a dire threat to world peace.

"Of all the revolting child cretins that trip through the endless scene of the American comic strips," he declared, fairly quivering with rage, "Little Orphan Annie is the one that I would like to strangle most. This desperate child, with her eternal cuteness, her unbearable moralizing, her sacred New-World kiddiness has now entered the field of international Hydrogen-Bomb Politics. . . . Little Orphan Annie's starry-eyed philosophy of the American way of life has thrived on the curls of this unctuous brat for 30 years. But her adolescent charms, her winks, her mincing curtsies have not, to my knowledge, hitherto proclaimed the policy that the best way to keep order in this world is to smash it flat. I suppose several million comic-strip addicts on the other side of the Atlantic from six to 60 years old will now believe in the policy of courage through fear."

The Detroit *Free Press*, however, found warm comfort in Warbucks' no-nonsense approach to foreign policy and voiced its respect for Gray, whom it described as "not a fabricator but a reporter. If he has a reportorial fault, it is understatement. . . . So far as we are concerned, Gray can hereafter go as far as he likes. We stand ready to believe him. Nothing he may do with Annie, Axel, Daddy Warbucks and the others will be held against him by us as preposterous. We will merely say to ourselves that Annie represents the people of this Country, Warbucks is Uncle Sam and Axel is what we are up against in the matter of Russia."

Incredibly, at the same time he was being branded a Fascist in

"WHAT A GIRL!"

London and a savior in Detroit, a woman in Southern California was composing a long letter to Norman Chandler, publisher of the Los Angeles *Times*, complaining about the "party line" she had detected in *Little Orphan Annie*. Her letter was forwarded to Gray, who wrote a lengthy reply to the woman's "refreshing" analysis:

For years I have been getting thousands of protests, but over 99 percent of them call me unprintable names, the mildest being 'dirty, filthy capitalist swine'! I have always been proud of those letters. Your letter is at least a change of pace. You are one of the very, very few that label me a Communist. Really, that is humor, in sort of a macabre way.

Naturally there are a lot of left-wing voters. I know a lot of them. All of them hate my insides. I in turn have despised Roosevelt and his socialist, or creeping communist, policies since 1932, and said so in my stuff, so far as I was allowed to do so. I despise Truman's efforts to carry on the socialization and eventual communizing of this country. I hate professional do-gooders with other people's money. I hate hypocrites. I dislike good people who scream that gambling is sin, but still believe that gambling is all right for church parties, or for anything that they feel is a 'worthy cause.' That's hardly Communism.

God knows I'm not trying to reform this system. But on the other hand, why be a stupid Pollyanna and preach that all judges and police are paragons of virtue, getting rich on their meager salaries? It simply isn't so. If we are going to worry so much about Communism, wouldn't it be a good thing to do a little local housecleaning under our own system?

Our system works fine, so far as I am concerned, except that we here seem vulnerable to socialist panaceas. So I have and shall continue to pound on the idea that the old-time way was the best for us—individual freedom, honest, hard work, and the chance for any man with the proper drive and decency to gain and hold wealth and power. By the same token I shall continue to preach my belief that anyone who is a congenital bum should be forced by necessity to work and earn a living— or starve. I feel there has been too damn much sentiment wasted in maudlin sympathy for the underprivileged—who as a rule are simply those who take that 'All men are created equal' thing too literally.

So long as we can fight off the creeping communism of socialism we will continue to be strong and rich. So long as we continue to be a Republic—and not the 'Democracy' that so many poor, misguided souls have been taught we are, we'll make out all right—in spite of Orphan Annie, eh?

Some of the other critics of Gray's comic strip had less philosophical concerns. When Annie and Sandy were mowed down by an automobile and their bodies tossed in the city dump, the managing editor of the Rochester *Democrat-Chronicle* voiced the "deep concern" of the paper's staff and readers that such a gruesome act had been depicted in a comic strip. It didn't help that the car had been driven by a doctor and his nurse, even if they were villains.

"The latest adventures of Annie have been the ultimate in horror and poor taste," the Rochester editor wrote to the Tribune syndicate. "Will you please let me, or our feature editor, know in advance when anything of so macabre a theme is contemplated? Dick Tracy in his goriest days could hardly tie Annie in her recent antics. We feel so strongly on this score that we contemplate dropping the strip until a bit of the blood is mopped from it."

Because of that and other complaints about too much violence, Annie and Sandy were hastily deposited in the home of a mildly retarded man named Simple Samson. Annie was soon on the mend, but had amnesia and couldn't even remember Sandy's name. The proof of Gray's sense of humor was his parody of *Little Orphan Annie* right in its own panels: He arranged for Samson to discover Annie's and Sandy's identities while reading *Little Orphan Annie* in the comic pages of the local paper. "Yep, that must be us!" Annie exclaimed when Samson showed it to her.

Annie's amnesia lasted more than a year, and through several adventures. Daddy, as usual, was halfway around the world and unaware of the perils she faced. He was shown one day reclining comfortably on the deckchair of his yacht, wondering out loud what his ward was up to. "She'll *always* be okay. What a girl! Never have to worry about her!" At that very moment, of course, she was facing death for the umpteenth time.

It often seemed that Gray's ultimate goal in life was to offend everybody at once. If that was the case, he came close to success in 1956 with a sequence on juvenile delinquency. The bellowing of outrage reached hurricane proportions. The story provoked angry editorials in union and religious publications, the syndicate's mailbag bulged with letters, and—most serious of all—a number of papers canceled their subscriptions to *Little Orphan Annie*.

The storm broke while the Grays were on a long motor tour of North America. Those annual trips had begun during the Depression and resumed after the war's gas rationing ended. It was Gray's way of keeping track of the public pulse. He stopped at roadside diners and gas stations, at farms, schools, tourist camps, hardware stores, and pharmacies, in small towns and big cities, making sure that the trials and triumphs of Annie were an accurate reflection of what was going on "out there."

"I get ideas traveling," Gray explained. "I meet people. You can't understand people sitting still in one place—you've got to keep up with them."

The idea for the series on teenage delinquency had been suggested to Gray, and the cartoonist began it on the trip, where he was "talking with cabdrivers, bartenders, teachers—anyone who will give him insight into the teenagers, including teenagers themselves," according to a statement by the Tribune syndicate's vice president, Maurice Reilly.

In the strip, Annie turned up on the tough side of a big city, where she got to know the local teenage punks, who were organized into a boys' gang called the Valentines and a girls' gang called the Witches. After winning their respect with her famous fast left, Annie dropped into the background and became an incidental character in a story about petty larceny, drug addiction, links between youth gangs and adult gangsters, and the uphill struggle by honest cops, their hands tied by "reformers," to break up the gangs.

It was a harsh series, even for Gray. During its course, a gang member named Junior delivered a sneering speech to his father, upbraiding him for knuckling under to the union that controlled the factory where he worked. Later, a rival gang broke into Junior's family's apartment, beat up his father, and were about to carve Junior up with switchblades when Annie blinded them with a fire extinguisher. Then, another gang member became a drug addict and killed a harmless panhandler for money to buy a fix. The cop on the beat was so enraged at that that he tracked down the junkie on his own time and kicked him to death. It was a far, far cry from the story of a little frizzy-haired girl who only wanted to leave the orphanage.

Organized labor called it "anti-union venom." An editorial in the *Oregon Labor Press*, widely reprinted in other labor publications, said: "With all the subtlety of a 40-ton locomotive, the strip compares unions to gangs of teenage juvenile delinquents. It is an outrage that this sort of tripe is being peddled to little children through a comic strip. Regular readers of the Orphan Annie strip may be angered by this anti-union outburst, but actually they won't be too surprised. Anyone who has read Daddy Warbucks' sermons on Unlimited Free Enterprise and his tirades against Creeping Socialism is well aware of Gray's extreme right-wing views. It's not surprising that he hates unions, too. Gray's prejudices are obvious enough to grown-up readers—but should he be allowed to poison the minds of little children?"

Labor found an ally in Msgr. George C. Higgins, whose column in the *Catholic Standard* on January 13, 1956, was headlined: " 'Tain't Funny, No More." Father Higgins wrote that *Annie* "has degenerated into a political tract with a demonstrably anti-union bias. It is calculated to leave the impression with umpteen millions of children, between the ages of 5 and 65, that all unions are a racket and a dangerous threat to the American way of life." The priest denounced Junior's insinuation that his father had been afraid not to join the factory union, "which says in the crudest possible way that this used to be a free country until the gangster-ridden unions came along and forced the workers to organize—or else.

"Few, if any, newspapers in the United States would have the gall to run this sort of propaganda in their editorial columns, yet hundreds of papers are blandly running it in the comic section," Father Higgins continued. "Surely there is something slightly ridiculous about a paper like the Washington *Post*, for example, which believes in unions, running a comic strip which says that unions are a form of gangsterism."

Among the newspapers that canceled *Little Orphan Annie* were the St. Louis *Globe-Democrat*, the *Ohio State Journal* in Columbus, the Syracuse *Post-Standard*, the Edmonton *Journal* in Canada and, according to *Time* magazine, "half a dozen other dailies from Buffalo to Salt Lake City."

"Annie's current continuity features teenage gangs, muggings, switchblade knives and language that we think does not fit into the type of newspaper the *Globe-Democrat* has been and intends to continue to be," the St. Louis editors explained in a front-page box.

"We regret having to dispossess her, but we could find nothing entertaining about the current continuity involving teenage wars and youthful hoodlumism," their counterparts in Syracuse echoed, adding that *Little Orphan Annie* would not be printed in the paper again "until the artist and syndicate put this soulful waif back into the kind of adventures that made her one of America's favorite comic-page personalities."

And a letter to *Time* from a reader in Columbus expressed the fear that Annie had "fallen in with the wrong crowd."

The bombardment of letters and editorials didn't particularly bother the syndicate, which had gotten used to the controversy Gray stirred up. But the fact that so many papers—eventually 30—had dropped *Little Orphan Annie* bothered them a great deal. Gray was

Right from the start, Annie was a feisty little girl. In this first Sunday comic strip, drawn in November 1924, Gray's orphan was depicted as basically a good kid trying to cope with a bad situation.

(*Above*) Harold Gray, a farmboy from Indiana, was Annie's creator. His original idea for a comic strip was a boy named "Little Orphan Otto." (*Top right*) Captain Joseph Medill Patterson, founder of the *Daily News,* thought Otto looked like a sissy. "Put a skirt on him and we'll call it *Little Orphan Annie,*" he suggested. (*Right*) Life wasn't easy for Annie at the "home" run by mean Miss Asthma.

YES, BUT NOT FOR YOU, YOUNG LADY— I JUST DISCOVERED YOU FAILED TO MAKE YOUR BED PROPERLY THIS MORNING SO YOU WILL EAT MUSH AND MILK IN THE KITCHEN—

GEE WHISKERS! THAT DOESN'T SEEM FAIR— WE ONLY HAVE ICE CREAM ABOUT ONCE A YEAR AND I LIKE IT BETTER 'N ANYTHING—

Mrs. Oliver Warbucks, a phony philanthropist, took Annie home "on trial" to impress her society pals with her charity.

One of the most memorable moments in comic-strip history came when Oliver Warbucks arrived home and found Annie living there. The munitions manufacturer and the little orphan took a shine to each other right away.

Among the most frequently asked questions over the years concerned Annie's vacant eyes and the red dress she wore almost all the time. Gray replied with a series of sketches in the Fifties.

"It does one's heart good·'"

"It does one's heart good when we see justice meted out properly, even though it has to be published on the funny page."

Praise for ORPHAN ANNIE from a column in The Call, Woonsocket, R. I.—the type of praise that reflects unparalleled popularity among readers, young and old. The adventures of this little tyke are followed by millions daily . . . Are your readers among them? If not, *now* is a good time to start!

For proofs and prices,

WRITE-PHONE-WIRE

The songs Annie has inspired include a finger-popping tune from the Twenties and the famous theme song from her radio show in the Thirties.

(facing page) *Little Orphan Annie was one of the Tribune Company Syndicate's most popular features, and was heavily promoted with advertisements aimed at newspaper editors.*

Daddy Warbucks was forever going off on mysterious "business trips," leaving Annie to fend for herself.

The first time Daddy went away, he was barely out the door when jealous Mrs. Warbucks sent Annie back to Miss Asthma's "home."

The radio program sponsored by Ovaltine during the Depression was one of the most popular shows on the air. Child star Shirley Bell played Annie.

To my friend
Orphan Annie
Shirley Bell

The show originated in the studios of station WGN in Chicago, where staff announcer Quinn Ryan often found himself surrounded by young fans. Shirley Bell is to his left, Allan Baruck, who played Annie's sidekick Joe Corntassle, is to his right.

Ovaltine gave away millions of hot-drink mugs, like the one on the left. In 1980, the company marked its 50th "Annie-versary" with a new mug. The Ovaltine container, too, underwent drastic changes.

Annie went to Hollywood twice in the Thirties. In 1932, RKO made a movie based on Gray's comic strip, starring 10-year-old Mitzi Green, who posed for Gray. A second movie was made in 1938 by Paramount. Both films bombed.

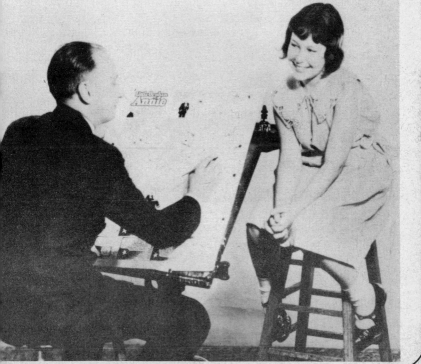

Like everyone else, Annie had her share of hard times in the Depression. She was always an optimist, though, and found some blessings to count at the end of 1932.

Gray had a firm rule against "happy endings." So even when things worked out fine for her friends, Annie always hit the road, heading off toward new adventures.

OH, MR. [...]OT- WE'RE [...]LL SO GLAD [...]OR YOU-

WE ALL KNEW _YOU_ NEVER _COULD_ HAVE COMMITTED SUCH A HORRIBLE CRIME-

[...]E ALL [...]D FAITH [...]N YOU-

THAT TERRIBLE MONSTER, HALK! UGH! I NEVER DID TRUST THAT MAN-

THANKS-

HUMPH! _MY_ PALS NOW, EH? OH, WELL--- HALK FOOLED SMARTER FOLKS THAN THEY ARE- THEY MEAN WELL- ONLY FAIR TO MEET THEM HALF-WAY- I NEVER WAS MUCH GOOD AT HOLDING A GRUDGE-

9-22-36

[W]HILE TRAMPING ALONG TOGETHER- HOW CAN THEY GUESS WHAT'S HAPPENED BACK IN BUTTERNUT?

GEE- IT SEEMS SORTA AS IF WE'RE RUNNIN' OUT ON POOR "UNCLE" JACK- BUT HE'S IN JAIL AND THERE'S NOT A THING WE COULD DO TO HELP HIM-

I'D STICK AROUND AND VISIT HIM AND TRY TO CHEER HIM UP- BUT THAT'D ONLY GET ME BACK INTO TH' COUNTY FARM- BR-R-R-- NOPE- I GUESS TH' FARTHER WE GET FROM BUTTERNUT, TH' BETTER-- EH, SANDY?

ARF!

HAROLD GRAY

Gray and his wife, Winifred, had no children, so they decorated their Christmas cards with pictures of Annie and Sandy.

Daddy Warbucks was Gray's alter ego, who could alternate between self-righteousness (left) and self-pity (right).

The characters in *Little Orphan Annie* went marching off to World War II in 1942 with everyone else. As usual, Daddy did things on his own term

Orphan Annie's Junior Commando Poster

(*Above*) The Junior Commando movement that began in Gray's comic strip sent thousands of youngsters digging through back yards, attics, and junkpiles for materials to feed the war machine.

Annie, Sandy, and Daddy were among the most easily identifiable of comic characters. Their portrait, with the suggested presence of Daddy's murderous henchmen, Punjab and the Asp, hung for many years in the New York offices of the Tribune syndicate.

Gray's characters also lent themselves easily to caricatures by his fellow cartoonists. Al Capp spoofed them in his own *Li'l Abner* comic strip, *Mad Magazine* wondered in 1960 what Annie would look like all grown up, and Harvey Kurtzman's *Little Annie Fanny* appeared monthly in *Playboy*.

"Whether you're rich, or whether you're poor, it's nice to have money!!"

—Old prove[rb]

Now Annie is young, so you hear!
Now Annie is young, so you hear!
But I am assertin'
That I know for certain
She's now in her 36th year!

I want every reader to kno[w]
The comics, they ain't nes[sa]
Ain't nessa—ain't nessa—
Ain't necessarily so!

12

Annie's appearance changed a lot over the years: she was short and cute in 1925, six months after Gray began drawing her; she was tall and had pupils by 1967, the year before Gray died; and didn't look much like herself at all in 1974, just before she became the only comic strip in history to go into reruns.

The original pen-and-ink drawings by Gray became collectors' items after he died. This one from 1925, personally authographed by Gray, shows Annie and Sandy one month after he arrived in the strip as a puppy—the only one of Gray's characters ever to grow up.

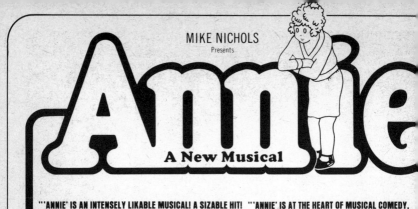

MIKE NICHOLS
Presents

Annie

A New Musical

Charles Strouse, Martin
Charnin, and Thomas
Meehan fashioned Gray's
characters into a Broadway
musical in 1977. They had a
tough time interesting
anyone else in the idea, but
after the show opened, it
became one of the biggest
hits in theater history, and a
real critics' choice.

In the original Broadway cast, Daddy Warbucks was played by Reid Shelton, Annie was Andrea McArdle, and Sandy was played by Sandy, a mutt rescued from the dogpound.

Veteran cartoonist Leonard Starr was chosen by the Tribune syndicate in 1979 for the important mission of resurrecting Annie as a comic strip.

ON STAGE

Starr had to change his style from the realism of his earlier strip, *On Stage*, but succeeded in plotting and drawing *Annie* where others had failed.

Like Gray, Starr was a meticulous researcher, and wanted *Annie* to be topical. For the first episode he was right on the money.

(*Facing page*) Other examples of *Annie* strips indicate Starr's ability to keep his stories interesting day after day.

The six "orphans" of the movie *Annie* had a cumulative age of 57 and filled set designer Dale Hennesy's $1 million New York "street" at the Burbank Studios, where much of *Annie* was filmed.

(*Facing page*) The interiors of Warbucks' "mansion" were filmed in the administrative building of Monmouth College in New Jersey, which had originally been built as a mansion for the president of F.W. Woolworth.

The distinguished British actor Albert Finney was cast as Warbucks in the movie *Annie*.

Aileen Quinn won Annie's red dress—and the plummest child role in years—from some 8,000 girls who auditioned in the greatest Hollywood talent hunt since the search for Scarlett O'Hara. Sandy had three understudies.

Carol Burnett plays Miss Hannigan (based on Gray's Miss Asthma) in the movie version of *Annie*.

Aileen Quinn as Annie saves Sandy from the cops in an early scene from the movie.

Almost 100 licensees put out
some 600 products for the
merchandising campaign that
Columbia Pictures and Rastar Films
organized for their production
of *Annie*. Among the products
are Annie dolls modeled on the
film characters produced by
Knickerbocker Toy Co., a board
game by Parker Brothers, and
children's pajamas.

contacted and ordered to send Annie and Sandy somewhere else—fast. At the time, he and Winifred were driving along the California coast. They stopped in Carmel, where Gray tore up six weeks' worth of work and spent nearly all his waking hours drawing a whole new set of strips as replacements for the delinquency series.

Among those who felt compelled to take potshots at *Little Orphan Annie*, particularly after the teen-gang episode, were scholars and intellectuals. They seemed to relish the prospect of reading all sorts of meaning into Gray's tea leaves.

In an article published in *America* magazine on December 8, 1956, a New Orleans English professor, Stephen P. Ryan, alerted readers to the "weighted and slanted campaign" to mold public opinion being conducted in the comic books and funny papers. Among the prime offenders, he announced, was "an ill-drawn, familiar feature known as Orphan Annie," whom he described as an "unpleasant child invariably accompanied by the most unintelligent of all comic-strip dogs, limited to a one-word vocabulary, 'Arf!'"

Daddy Warbucks, in the professor's opinion, was "a blustering show-off (who) takes precious poor care of his relatives. Despite his great financial acumen, he is too stupid to keep track for more than two or three weeks at a time of a child he presumably loves."

Another character who offended Ryan was Collar John, an itinerant clergyman who showed up in the middle of the teen-gang sequence to open a storefront mission in the toughest neighborhood in the city. His arrival was hailed in Tribune syndicate promotion material as "a constructive and memorable contribution to the world's most popular medium." But Ryan saw little of the Christian spirit in Collar John's methods for putting people on the path of righteousness: "Our man of the cloth wins his converts by his ability to knock the stuffing out of the local thugs and his amazing knowledge, acquired as a wartime commando, of some of the more spectacular and unorthodox methods of subduing an opponent."

And Ryan didn't think youth in general had been very well served by exposure to Annie's adventures on the wrong side of town. "During the past year, much of the background was centered about the problem of juvenile delinquency in our cities. Of course, virtue triumphed and the evildoers were punished; but in the process we were treated to an astonishing display of the operations of dope pushers, switchblade artists, crime-syndicate bosses and the legendary prostitute with 'a heart of gold.' Throw in some venal policeman and crooked politicians and you have a delightful picture for the edification of the young."

A far more intellectual analysis of *Little Orphan Annie* had been offered in *Harper's* one year earlier by Ignatius Mattingly. He took the view that, like "jazz, the movies, dime novels, hillbilly ballads, even television," comic strips were destined to become—if they had not already—a serious art form, requiring serious criticism, which he engaged in forthwith.

Mattingly found parallels between Annie's constant quest for Daddy and the Greek legend of Telemachus' search for Odysseus, "with whom Daddy Warbucks has much in common. Warbucks is Capitalism, and more particularly, Capitalism of the old-fashioned type, what might be called Bird-dog Capitalism. Warbucks has vast holdings, quasi-magical powers, a Nietzschean contempt for regularly constituted authority, and apparent immortality, like a corporation.

"Orphan Annie, on the other hand—weak, persecuted, continually sorry for herself—is Capitalism in the modern manner, in search of its former glories. Like Daddy Warbucks, Annie is impatient of Community Regulation (symbolized by cops), yet she is always on the alert to chisel a handout (subsidy, tariff advantage). Annie herself sums up the spirit of Kenneldog Capitalism in her line: 'We've never yet been 'pendent on anybody . . . at least not very much, if we could help it.' "

Mattingly's high-flown, and somewhat flawed, dissection of the situation is in sharp contrast to the straightforward words of Al Capp, who drew *L'il Abner*. Capp came to Gray's defense in the early Fifties when a movement got underway to stamp out comics, like *Little Orphan Annie*, that depicted violence and lawbreaking.

"This is a fan letter," Capp wrote to Gray. "You've done a damned good job blasting the phony 'anti-comic-book crusade.' If more cartoonists were aware of the danger of this thing, we might squash it. These phonies are willing to come out boldly against the comic book and comic-strip publishers because they are the least organized, the least politically powerful, the least offensive. They are horrified, confused, shocked when you demand that they apply precisely the same standards to the great, organized, powerful mass distributors of horror, sex, crime entertainment. If you insist that the do-gooders include radio and movies in their sanctimonious 'crusade,' the whole thing falls apart of its own weight. Most effective of all is the sort of stuff you've been doing. Thanks for it."

Gray's reply to Capp revealed his volcanic fury over the attempts—some of them by then successful—to put a muzzle on him: "Since even the harmless old platitudes concerning honesty, virtue and hard work have become political dynamite, you are about the only comic artist left with the guts and set-up to say anything in the strip. They sure as hell have me hog-tied now, but good. And now any suggestion of violence in a strip seems to be good for suspension, if not a cancellation, with most of our new breed of prissy editors. Soon I presume it will be illegal to print even reports of murders, or crimes of any sort, in a newspaper. Sometimes I get disgusted with the whole damn business. But it's a living, eh?''

A full decade later, Gray hadn't softened a bit. "Sweetness and light—who the hell wants it?" he snarled in an interview with *Time* for an article on Annie's 40th anniversary. "What's news in the newspaper? Murder, rape and arson. That's what stories are made of."

The *Time* anniversary story pronounced Annie "one of the most durable, reactionary, humorless and lucrative little brats in the history of the funnies," and reported that Gray's earnings from her amounted to $5 million. That figure may have been too high, but probably not by much. There was no disguising the fact that Gray was a wealthy man. In the early Fifties, he had been offered—and had accepted—a position as a director of a new bank then being formed, the First National Bank of Westport.

George Longstreth, the bank executive who had invited Gray onto the board, many years later described the cartoonist as a "rough diamond. He could swear like a trooper, but he was a very kind, gentle man. And very generous." But Longstreth was one of only a small number of people who got to know Gray very well over the years.

"He shunned the limelight," Longstreth recalled in an interview in 1981. "Very few people knew him and his wife. He wanted it that way. When they traveled, he became very upset if someone found out who he was. One time we met them for lunch in Jamaica aboard their cruise ship. My wife introduced him to the captain as the man who drew *Little Orphan Annie*, and he almost took her head off right then and there."

Longstreth got the impression that Gray's favorite place, besides his drawing board and the open road, was in the company of other newspaper people. "When he got together with a bunch of his cronies, he used to love to reminisce about the criminals in Chicago, where he was a reporter during the Capone era. He didn't talk very much about the comic strip."

Another Westport area resident who got to know Gray was Jud Hurd, the publisher of the magazine *Cartoonist ProFiles*. Hurd had first met Gray as a young man back in the late Thirties. When he moved to Westport with his wife and son in 1964, Hurd renewed the acquaintance and the two families went out to lunch together frequently.

"He wasn't a mixer," Hurd said of Gray in a 1981 interview. "He was putting in 10 or 12 hours a day working on the strip. He was a very private individual and I always thought of him as being a great deal like Daddy Warbucks. He was the individualist type who had started working in Chicago during those rip-snorting days. I considered him a hard-driving, hard-talking individual that I don't imagine would be very sympathetic to the present system of thinking that everybody deserves to be carried from the cradle to the grave at the government's expense. He felt you had to make it on your own, and if you didn't, tough.

"He liked to tell stories about the old days in Chicago. You had the feeling, although he was a slender individual and not particularly tall, that there was an inner force, which is why I always thought of him as Daddy Warbucks. He was the type of fellow that, having become extremely successful in early life and maintaining it throughout, had an enormous amount of confidence. It didn't come out in bragging, but you had the feeling that here was somebody that had made it and made it big.

"I think what you found in *Annie* was exactly how he felt about the world," Hurd said. "I'm sure the criticism didn't bother him a bit."

Gray appeared to wear the cloak of his success comfortably, but not ostentatiously. The houses where he and Winifred lived in the Westport area got progressively smaller over the years, and the Chrysler Imperial they owned was not so much a status symbol as a practical, sturdy vehicle to carry them on their grueling cross-country trips, which were putting up to 40,000 miles a year on the odometer.

On one such jaunt to Southern California in 1958, they bought a second home in La Jolla, a seaside resort community just north of San Diego. "We came here to see some people," Gray explained to a reporter from the San Diego *Union*. "One day I said to my wife, 'Let's see a real estate agent just to kill time.' Here we are." He dubbed the place "Western Headquarters" and set up his drawing board in the den, facing a huge picture window that overlooked the Pacific Ocean. From then on, the Grays spent summers in Westport and winters in La Jolla.

Neither the balmy climate of Southern California nor his advancing age mellowed Gray's disposition in the least. Free from the restraints of public print in his private letters, he could be virulent when provoked, which didn't take much. When a printer's strike shut down the big Manhattan newspapers for 114 days in 1962, the unionized clerical workers at the syndicate honored the picket lines and refused to go to work. Management employees were able to get all the features, including *Little Orphan Annie*, out to subscribers. But Gray took the walkout as a personal affront. His reaction to it, contained in a letter he wrote from La Jolla to syndicate manager Mollie Slott, was a catalog of complaints from a man who hadn't had any real grounds to complain about anything for years.

"So now the stupid grease monkeys have struck the paper and all the rest of the clerks and clowns and goldbricks with the mental power of field hands are out, too," he wrote. "That's great! Never in my life have I ever known a really competent newspaper man who needed or was helped by a Guild or Union. The only people who ever have been helped by the union on a paper are the dull hacks, the office workers, clerks, etc.—the 'common people,' and by God they are common. These strikes now remind me of rats gnawing holes in the ship that, if it sinks, will drown them. The bastards thrown out of work by such wrecked paper should starve to death. It was a terribly hard job you did, but it seems to me it proved how completely unnecessary a lot of the help really is and how well a few *workers* could handle the operation and how easily the goldbricks could be dispensed with. Aren't some of the staff there old enough now in service to be retired?"

Gray went on to berate the syndicate's sales representatives for not pushing hard enough for subscribers, but noted that he himself was working "very hard all the time" so he and Winifred could take the time to travel to Mexico. He added the self-contradictory remark, "I detest Mexico and most Mexicans, though we always get along all right when down there."

All in all, it wasn't a very flattering portrait of the father of America's favorite little girl. Its harsh, cynical tone belied the cheerful optimism that had buoyed the followers of *Little Orphan Annie* through the years.

Although most of the letters that arrived in Gray's mailbox by the truckload over the years had to do with something specific that was going on in *Little Orphan Annie* at the time, there were many letters about the general aspects of the strip and its characters. The most frequently asked questions were about Annie's pupil-less eyes, her limited wardrobe, and her perennial youth.

Typical was the letter sent in by a dozen employees of a Kansas City car dealership in 1942: "Why don't you make eyes that look like eyes on your Orphan Annie cartoons? We have wished so many times that you could make a dot in each eye to bring them to life. And in reply to a question about your Orphan Annie cartoons, some of us said we did not even read them because they have no eyes. Sure wish you would give it a trial and see how they look. We like the funnies, but we do like for them to have eyes."

Gray did tinker briefly with Annie's eyeballs, giving them pupils for a while in the late Forties. The result, after all those years of vacant sockets, was that she looked funny. Among those who didn't like her new look was a New York art director, who wrote: "I have noticed that you have introduced small dots of pupils into the eyes of your characters and feel that it is a mistake. This device may give direction and possibly expression to the eyes, but it seems to me that you had successfully built up an interesting style with the deadpan eyes you formerly used. I feel it is an unhappy decision. I also suspect that you are a little undecided about it yourself since you have done it rather halfheartedly and inconsistently. Maybe you have been wondering whether readers notice these things. This is your answer."

Annie's age was a constant subject of reader mail. A woman in Bayonne, New Jersey, sent a postcard in 1935: "From a *Daily News* dated in 1928, a picture was shown to me of Orphan Annie making purchases all by herself and quite a fair-sized girl. How is it now that she is a small girl receiving a dollie from Santa Claus? Is she an imbecile?"

Gray gave his definitive answer to that burning question in a promotion piece in 1949 for the Tribune syndicate: "Many of the readers think she should grow up—and I suppose run me out of gas in a few short years. No, she'll stand still, while the kids who read her doings grow up and new ones arrive, I hope, to take their places in her audience."

In another question-and-answer package assembled by the syndicate, Gray was asked if, like many of the readers of Annie, he ever felt like "wringing her neck."

"Sure! Frequently!" he answered. "Every time she comes up with some crazy idea that gets me into trouble. For instance: her silly yammering that it's American to WORK for a living, save money and be self-supporting. Rustic drivel for years now, of course. And she thinks it's always open season on windbag politicians. I TELL her that's editorializing, but she always has an answer. 'Then why not make up the paper right?' she snips. 'Run the comics on the editorial page, and editorials on the comic page!' But she's a good kid at heart—and a dandy meal ticket, believe me."

In 1948, a Los Angeles man wrote in: "A few months ago I read in *Look* magazine an article concerning Little Orphan Annie. It stated that after Easter, Annie was going to be transformed into a slinky piece of whistle bait. It also stated that Sandy would be shot. Well— we are waiting. If, for no other reason than to please your readers, please shoot someone, Sandy or Annie."

Another letter, signed "A Sufferer," arrived at the syndicate. "Thank God for that fellow who wishes Little Orphan Annie ill," it began. "Now there is a really intelligent person. That little juvenile delinquent should be shot. Why doesn't someone put her out of her misery? She can't be happy, she is always in trouble, never goes to school, hasn't any decent clothes, and is an addle-brained nincompoop. She should be in prison, the little stinker. I hope she gets what is coming to her. The only person in the whole dumb thing that is any good is that poor stupid dog Sandy. I say stupid for if he had any brains at all he would have let Annie get hit by a car long ago. You had better print this or I will stop reading *Little Orphan* (Thank God) *Annie* altogether."

And then there were those who were always ready to correct Gray's mistakes. "I'm a little tired of seeing Daddy Warbucks disappear and periodically leave Annie broke as a result," wrote a lawyer in New York. "Trust-fund plans give the beneficiary a guaranteed income for life. I therefore am willing to set up, free of charge to the parties concerned for my services, a trust fund by Daddy Warbucks for the benefit of Annie. P.S. I would do this for the Asp and Punjab also. P.P.S. At any rate, something has to be done, as I just cannot stand the thought of Annie being left on the rocks next time Daddy leaves town, nor can my little seven-year-old niece at whose insistence I write."

His fellow cartoonists enjoyed many a laugh at the expense of Gray and his creation. Annie's distinctive mannerisms and appearance made her the butt of some good-natured ribbing in other comics. One Sunday's installment of *L'il Abner* was entitled "Sweet Fanny Gooney." It had a fat, bald-headed creature named Daddy Sawbucks, who thought he had bumped off his creepy orphan sidekick until she popped up toward the end, announced that her life had been spared by the "Vote for Landon" button that she always pinned to her chest, and drilled Daddy full of holes with a machine gun.

Walt Kelly did a takeoff called "Little Arf an' Nannie" for his *Pogo* comic strip.

But the most consistently done—and most widely distributed—was the comic strip *Little Annie Fanny*, published in the back of *Playboy* magazine beginning in 1961. It was created by Harvey Kurtzman, the founder of *Mad* magazine, which had also done many spoofs of *Little Orphan Annie* in the Fifties. Annie Fanny was, in Kurtzman's words, "a zaftig female blonde" who continually got herself into one sexual misadventure after another but was always saved by her amazing naiveté. After the first few years, *Little Annie Fanny* moved on to other topics and became much less a direct takeoff of *Little Orphan Annie*.

When *Time* did its 40th-anniversary piece on *Little Orphan Annie*,

Gray told the magazine he was through with politics for good. "You'll get cut no matter which side you're on," he said. That signaled a change in targets, not in tactics. In 1965, he had the nation's mental-health establishment tearing its hair out over a sequence he later labeled "The Crazy Episode" in his personal papers.

He tossed Annie and Daddy into a private insane asylum in a remote section of the country. Its founder was an evil—and phony—headshrinker named Dr. LeQuaque, who had the look of a deranged Sigmund Freud. The place was more of a clink than a clinic, as indicated by the cook's description of one of the inmates seen shuffling meekly around the grounds: "Rich guy. Golddigger wife liked his money, sick o' *him*! Got a couple guys t' certify he was '*mentally ill*'! He didn't agree, so they had him arrested! He got five days o' 'treatment.' Then y'think he got a hearing? Ha! The psychiatrist said t' bring him t' court would be 'injurious to th' patient'! So-o-o, there he is, from now on, while his wife and her pals split up th' loot!"

Needless to say, psychiatrists, psychologists, and everyone else working in the field of mental health went berserk. Long before Gray exposed Dr. LeQuaque and shut down his operation, letters were streaming into newspaper offices from Maine to Hawaii.

The Hartford *Courant* yanked Annie out of its pages and assured its readers that citizens in Connecticut "can't be railroaded" into mental institutions the way Gray had shown. The Dallas *Times Herald* labeled the sequence "irresponsible propaganda," but continued to print the strip because "even misguided Orphan Annies are entitled to a viewpoint without censorship." The Los Angeles *Times*, however, printed an editorial chiding the "white-coats" for their strong reaction, noting that perhaps "their patients' anxieties are rubbing off on them. A few sessions on each others' couches might be good for the anxious mental specialists. Is there a Greek name for the disorder that would be defined as 'to be frightened by a comic strip'?"

Typically, Gray shrugged the whole thing off. "I'm not crusading," he told *Time*. "I'm doing a script. I know some editors are writing editorials saying it couldn't happen in their states. But it can be done. The main thing is that I had to get Daddy Warbucks into a jam. This is a believable jam."

As always, there were lighter moments. Once, Annie and Sandy were killed in a plane crash. Everybody knew they weren't really dead, of course, but for two agonizing weeks her crumpled body lay motionless in a swamp as Sandy licked her face and barked frantically to revive her. The drama was so compelling that the Long Beach, California, *Independent Press Telegram* ran a contest in response to a letter it had received asking how Annie and Sandy could have survived the plane crash without so much as a parachute. The paper called upon its readers to "solve the mystery of the decade and earn money in the process." First prize, for the best solution in 100 words or less, was $25.

The suggestions ranged from the mundane to the bizarre: Annie and Sandy had been in the tail section of the plane and had floated safely down with it, or riding on the emergency door; Sandy whirled his tail like a helicopter; Annie's dress opened up like a parachute; she grabbed hold of an umbrella; Superman, or Thor, or sky divers, or a "giant duck" carried them safely to earth.

The best answer didn't offer any solution at all, but remarked: "What a sad state of affairs this world must be in if we *need* an explanation for any of Annie's escapes. May she live on and on!"

Unfortunately, that sentiment was waning among newspaper editors. The same year the Long Beach paper ran its contest, the Cincinnati *Enquirer* tried to drop *Little Orphan Annie*, but was forced to reinstate it in the face of strong support from readers. The *Daily Oklahoman* learned the same lesson two years later. "Leaving *Annie* out of the paper, it appears, is akin to omitting the score of the World Series," the *Oklahoman* said in a story announcing her impending return after a very brief absence from the comic pages. One paragraph near the bottom of that story, though, foretold the fact that she would not always be so sorely missed: "All of the complaints came from grown-ups, mostly men. The kids apparently didn't care, or at least they weren't upset enough to register a complaint."

Annie's fans were getting older, and though she kept making new ones, they were outnumbered by youngsters who preferred the newer comic strips that relied more on quick laughs than on carefully developed plots and characterizations. A Houston *Post* survey of its readers taken in the mid-Sixties found Charles Schulz's *Peanuts* to be the overwhelming favorite of comic-strip readers of nearly every age. Way down in 15th place was *Little Orphan Annie*, which the survey found to be the favorite strip only of those between the ages of 70 and 99. Among readers who were 19 or younger—the next generation of newspaper readers—Annie ranked 24th.

A similar conclusion was reached in a reader poll conducted by the Los Angeles *Times* in 1966. On the basis of the results, the paper's editor, Nick B. Williams, ordered *Little Orphan Annie* out of the *Times*.

"Some of the older comics began to sag," Williams recalled in an interview some years later. "The time came when *Little Orphan*

Annie dipped below a certain point, and that was it." At the same time, Williams canceled *Dick Tracy* and *L'il Abner*, and for the same reason.

"After I killed it, I happened to be in a meeting with the publisher, Norman Chandler," Williams said. "After the meeting, he came up to me and said, 'Why did you kill *Little Orphan Annie?*' I told him about the reader poll and how the new comics seemed to be more popular. 'Dammit,' he said to me, 'it was my favorite comic strip!' Of course, if he'd ordered me to put it back in the paper, I would have. But he didn't. He registered his complaint, just like everyone else."

Williams stuck to his guns in the face of letters such as this one, which spoke eloquently for Annie's many followers: "I have subscribed to the *Times* since coming to California in 1929, and during all of that time, I have followed the fortunes (and misfortunes) of Orphan Annie. Now it appears that the strip has been deleted from the comic page, being replaced by a new strip which must have been drawn by a fourth grader for others of that age. *Little Orphan Annie* was a classic among comic strips. Her daily struggle to survive with only very occasional aid from Daddy Warbucks was an epic, and we always looked forward to the next episode, confident that she would somehow solve any problem, either by judo or smoke signals or other clever stratagem. So, we protest its discontinuance, and ask that it be restored to your pages."

Even a piece by the *Times'* own columnist, Paul Coates, headlined "A Lament for Annie," couldn't bring her back.

"Something fine and decent has gone out of my life," Coates wrote. "They've taken away Orphan Annie. Tossed out with no visible means of support, only one dress to her name, and a frizzy coiffure still in a state of electric shock from an abortive permanent wave way back in the Twenties. Annie had what she and I would have called, in the old days, 'real moxie.' Orphan Annie represented the wholesome, All-American girl. She could hitch a ride on a freight train, swim a swamp, kick a tramp, or hold off a ragtag army of bearded, greasy, bomb-throwing foreigners. It's a dismal commentary on modern taste. We no longer have room in the literary scene for the homely, old-fashioned philosophy of a pre-puberty child who is wiser in many ways than even Mary Worth."

There was no reader survey to blame for the cancellation in June 1968 of *Little Orphan Annie* in the Greensboro, North Carolina, *Daily News. Annie* and *Dick Tracy* were both dropped "with reluctance," the paper's editors said, because of their "constant exploitation and advocacy of violence."

Tracy's creator, 67-year-old Chester Gould, told *Time* that his strip only reflected society's never-ending "battle against crime. We have to resort to violence to protect ourselves from evil."

Annie's creator, 74-year-old Harold Gray, was for once silent, having died of cancer the month before.

Chapter 7

"ANNIE WILL BE MISSED"

Daddy was dying. All through the spring of 1968, he grew weaker as the mysterious disease that gripped his body took its terrible toll. A tearful Annie and Sandy were at his side, as were Punjab and the Asp. This time there was no cure, it seemed. Daddy's time was growing short.

Harold Gray was dying. He'd known for more than a year that he had cancer and that there was little hope for a cure. His time, too, was running out.

Folded inside the pages of his diary was a newspaper clipping that described a new method for the treatment of cancer. It wasn't to do him any good in the end, but a similar "cure" did allow Daddy to outlive his creator, despite what some observers still regard as Gray's plan to have Warbucks' death coincide with his own.

The last entry in Gray's diary, written in a weak, trembling hand, was on May 6. It recorded the dialogue for the strip scheduled for publication 10 weeks later, on July 21. Three days later, he died in a bed at Scripps Hospital at La Jolla.

His death came as a complete surprise to Arthur Laro, president of the Tribune syndicate at the time. Laro was informed of it by a phone call from Winifred Gray. "He had not let us know that he was ill," Laro recalled. "Although I had noticed that his lines were not as true."

It's rare for a successful comic strip to go to the grave with its creator. A popular strip is a valuable commodity to a newspaper syndicate, which will do almost anything to keep it going. *Little Orphan Annie* still had hundreds of papers on its subscription list despite the defections in the preceding years. It was one of the biggest money-makers in the Tribune syndicate's stable.

When Gray's own mentor, Sidney Smith, had been killed in an automobile accident in 1935, his shoes were filled by Gus Edson, who kept *The Gumps* going for another 20 years. Likewise, *Mutt and Jeff, Gasoline Alley, Blondie*, and *Bringing Up Father*, all immensely popular—and profitable—strips, went on after the deaths of Bud Fisher, Frank King, Chic Young, and George McManus.

Comic-strip characters take on a life of their own. They are so familiar—and the artists who draw them so obscure—that their public rarely notices when they change hands. But there are some strips that are the product of such individual imagination that they cannot be continued. The best example was Walt Kelly's *Pogo*. Another example, as the syndicate would discover, was Harold Gray's *Little Orphan Annie*.

Laro never lent any credence to the theory that Daddy's illness was a reflection of Gray's own, or that Gray's plan was for *Little Orphan Annie* to die with him. "For one thing," Laro said, "Warbucks was always in danger. That he was ill didn't cause any concern in the office. For another, Gray was a very strong-willed man. He wouldn't have thrown in the towel."

Regardless, on the day he died the syndicate had only a few weeks to either find a successor or cancel the strip. "It was too valuable a property to give up," Laro said. "We had to make every effort to continue it."

The first crack at it went to the most logical successor to Gray—his cousin, Robert Leffingwell, who had been his assistant for many years. He wanted to do it, and tried to pick up the strip where Gray had left off. But over the years his main responsibilities had been lettering and backgrounds. When it came to putting it all together, he couldn't seem to make it come out right.

"I was praying that he could, but he could not," Laro said. "His work just didn't measure up."

The syndicate then played beat the clock. Laro asked a staff artist, Henry Arnold, to draw *Little Orphan Annie* and the general manager, Henry Raduta, to write the plot for it for a couple of weeks while he lined up a new team.

The new artist was Philip "Tex" Blaisdell, who had worked on many prominent strips over the years—*Prince Valiant, On Stage, Juliet Jones*, and others. "I was employed to forge it," he later said candidly. He did so, and in most opinions, very successfully. "Nobody could tell the difference between when Gray left off and I began," Blaisdell said proudly.

Laro asked Elliott Caplin, Al Capp's brother and a very successful comic-strip writer, to plot *Little Orphan Annie*. Caplin's credits at that point included *Abby and Slats*, *Juliet Jones*, and *Dr. Kildare*. Having disliked both Gray's strips and his politics over the years, Caplin was reluctant. But with a very large sum of money dangling in front of him, he finally agreed—but only on the condition that politics be avoided entirely.

"Our political philosophies were about as far apart as anyone's could get," Caplin said in an interview. "I didn't think I could do justice to the Harold Gray point of view. So I wrote charming, fascinating character stories."

Blaisdell and Caplin worked on *Little Orphan Annie* together for nearly six years, during which time the strip's subscription list dwindled steadily down. Their income from it reached the point where it simply wasn't worth it to continue. Caplin left in August 1973, and Blaisdell departed at the end of the year.

"It got to the point where we were losing papers like mad," Blaisdell said in an interview. "I was putting in 70 hours a week and earning less than two hundred dollars."

The blame for the erosion of *Little Orphan Annie* fell mainly on Caplin. His avoidance of political themes eliminated a vital element of the strip, it was felt. But Caplin did not agree.

"I worked my ass off," he said several years later. "I did the very best I could. It would be stupid to think I would deliberately harm a property that was paying me. I think it was losing its audience anyway. Inevitably, that happens with all continuity strips."

Little Orphan Annie became a true orphan in every sense of the word. It was passed briefly over to another artist and writer, but they, too, struck out. Annie got to be a weird-looking creature with an indescribable hairdo, hanging around with a bunch of hippies(!) who rode around in a psychedelic van, and whose chief nemesis was a big businessman (!!) who sold infected oysters to unsuspecting seafood restaurants.

"Horrible things have happened to Little Orphan Annie," a Washington *Post* feature writer declared. "Leapin' lizards, she looks awful! Her hairdo is a mess! Her politics, once rightist-righteous, have gone all liberal and squishy! Her head has grown! Her body's shrunk! She changes sizes from frame to frame. The tyke has lost her tart, her tough talk and her instinct for adventure. Sufferin' sunfish! She's lost her looks, her voice, her gumption and her soul."

More and more readers complained, and the list of subscribers to

"ANNIE WILL BE MISSED"

Little Orphan Annie kept shrinking. In early 1974, a 26-year-old Boston artist named David Lettick took over the strip. He both wrote it and drew it, and for the first time it bore a signature other than Gray's. It also bore a lot of hate mail from readers who were fit to be tied by his rendition of Annie. Lettick described her as "younger, cuter, and perhaps a little plumper" than Gray's girl. But the letters that arrived at the syndicate office had other adjectives for what he had done.

"What has happened to Little Orphan Annie?" demanded the Little Orphan Annie Asylum Society and the Sandy Kennel Club. "Poor child! Who is the new cartoonist who draws like a nursery-school dropout? The Asp should stalk him with a dirk. Swish! Punjab should make him disappear. Poof! Sandy should fang him on the seat of his britches. Arf! We are certain all Annie lovers who have suffered through hundreds of misadventures with her over many years believe that she and Sandy would find greater warmth and shelter, and a better home, at somebody else's drawing board."

A woman writing from Tulsa, Oklahoma, was only slightly more charitable. "My husband and I have been talking about how horrible the strip has been recently. We wouldn't go so far as to say the cartoonist should be fired immediately, but suggest he be given a chance to study previous cartoonists' work; and if he can't do a good job, he'd better look for another line of work. These characters bear only a slight resemblance to Annie and Sandy, in other words they are 'gross.'"

Lettick lasted only three months. Then the Tribune syndicate did something that had never been attempted before: it put *Little Orphan Annie* into reruns. It happened on Monday, April 22, 1974, when strips originally drawn by Harold Gray in 1936 appeared in the papers that still subscribed to *Little Orphan Annie*.

"Why we didn't think of this before I don't know," Robert S. Reed, the new syndicate president, said at the time. "It fits perfectly the current mood of nostalgia for the good things of the past."

The vintage strips were selected by a recently retired newspaper editor who, ironically, had been the one to cancel *Little Orphan Annie* at his own paper some years before. But after poring over five years of Gray's daily and Sunday panels, he began to think he'd made a big mistake earlier. "I'm amazed," he remarked. "The story line is strong and clear. The characters are sharply identified by appearance and by name. The only four-letter words are those like work and love and hope and fear. And Gray doesn't tease me for days while I wait for a development—his stories more than move, they gallop."

Other editors agreed. The subscription list for *Little Orphan Annie* grew by about 100 papers, making it one of the most widely distributed comic strips in America—drawn by a dead man in a long-gone era.

Readers, too, were enthusiastic. "To see Annie once again is a real pleasure," said a letter to the Los Angeles *Times*—one of the papers that picked up the "new" strips. "It's good to have Orphan Annie back in our time of troubles to take justice once more in her 50-year-old pre-pubescent little hands," said another.

The *Times'* editors knew they'd really hit the nail on the head when the old, familiar hate mail began arriving, too. "Isn't it bad enough to spiral downward from recession to depression without regressing to *Little Orphan Annie* all over again?" asked a Beverly Hills reader. "The blank-eyed 'good guys' in the strip always prevail by taking the law into their own hands, bringing some horrible violence to the 'bad guys.' Or else Daddy Warbucks arrives with a last-minute payoff. Or both. If the police are never around when needed, couldn't we at least have a truant officer? And just what is Warbucks' relationship to Annie? If he is any kind of legal guardian he is guilty of child neglect, since he is never around to bail Annie out of predicaments until the last ray of hope is gone. If he is not a legitimate guardian, he must be a dirty old man. Why doesn't he locate and marry Annie's mother to preserve appearances? I wonder if Sandy has a dog license."

But the general reaction was overwhelmingly favorable. A readership poll taken by the Buffalo *Evening News* in 1975 found that 75 percent of its comics fans wanted the old Annie strips kept in the paper. "Human nature never needs updating," one reader commented.

The Tribune syndicate's grand experiment went along nicely for two years, but at some point all good things must end, even the second time around. In March 1976, the New York *Daily News* dealt *Little Orphan Annie* the unkindest cut of all when it announced it was dropping the strip that had first appeared in its pages 52 years before. "For a while, these reruns made sense, considering the nostalgia craze," said a spokesman for the paper. "But even reruns run their course, and we feel these have, too."

In the moving "obituary" for the strip, Sunday Editor Worth Gatewood wrote that during the half-century they had journeyed across the pages of the *Daily News*, "Annie and Sandy triumphed over every adversity, and survived every peril except one: the death in 1968 of their creator. Gray's deceptively simple drawing and his complex story line—part adventure, part pathos, part morality play—eluded those who had tried to keep *Little Orphan Annie* going.

"Annie was a paragon, or maybe a parody, of all those virtues now regarded as simplistic early American: pluck, enterprise, honest and rugged individualism, and she needed all of them to get out of the lurches in which Daddy Warbucks was forever leaving her. But even if the villains nailed Annie into a barrel of broken glass and sent her bobbing downstream toward Niagara Falls, the readers knew she would survive. As in all morality plays, good always triumphed over evil. And like other remembrances of life in a simpler era, Annie will be missed."

The Washington *Post* dropped *Little Orphan Annie* on the same day. And although some 200 papers continued to publish Annie's recycled adventures, it looked like the final curtain was about to fall on Harold Gray's little girl.

Meanwhile, at a very small, very old theater in Connecticut, far from the bright lights of Broadway, the curtain was about to go up on a shaky, tentative summer production: a new musical based on the comic strip *Little Orphan Annie*.

Chapter 8

"THE WORST IDEA I'D EVER HEARD"

In all the hundreds of newspaper and magazine articles that have been written about "Annie" since it opened on Broadway in April of 1977, barely a handful don't contain somewhere in them the words: "Leapin' lizards!" Those two words, the only ones in the whole show written by Harold Gray, are spoken just once. They're a symbol of the vast gulf between Gray's comic strip and the musical fashioned from it by Martin Charnin, Thomas Meehan, and Charles Strouse.

Annie was no more a staged version of *Little Orphan Annie* than all the attempts by Caplin, Blaisdell, Lettick, and the others were the genuine continuation of Gray's lifetime work. The comic strip and the musical were apples and oranges, almost from the beginning.

The beginning was Christmas 1971. The last few shopping days found a man named Martin Charnin bustling along Fifth Avenue in New York, ducking into one store after another to buy last-minute presents. One of them was the Doubleday bookstore, where Charnin, an actor/writer/director spotted a large volume on the remainder counter. It was titled *Arf! The Life and Hard Times of Little Orphan Annie*, and it was a collection of Gray's daily strips, chosen at random from the years 1935 through 1945.

In what has since become a minor legend in show business, Charnin bought the book for a friend who had an interest in pop culture, and because he was in a hurry told the salesclerk not to bother wrapping it. He took the book home and began to casually thumb through it. Sometime in the middle of that night, he fell asleep. When he woke up he had the idea for a Broadway musical. It was just as well he didn't suspect then what a long and arduous journey it would be to opening night six years later.

The first stop was the offices of the Tribune syndicate, to secure the performing rights to *Little Orphan Annie.*

"The rights were not difficult to get," Charnin recalled in an interview 10 years later. "I was confronted with some dancing around that Hanna-Barbera was doing about wanting to make it a Saturday morning kids' cartoon feature. The syndicate agreed to give me the option for 12 months, with a six-month extension." That gave him 18 months in which to put a show together and get it on a Broadway stage. In retrospect, Charnin admitted, that timetable proved "wildly optimistic."

He wanted only to write the lyrics and direct, so he called his friend Tom Meehan, a writer for magazines and television who'd worked with him on an Emmy Award-winning television special for Anne Bancroft called—of all things—"Annie: The Women in the Life of a Man."

Meehan's first involvement in the musical came, he recalled in an article in the New York *Times*, "on a bleak afternoon in early January of 1972, when I had a phone call from Charnin. He had an idea for a musical he wanted me to write the book for" (the "book" of a musical is the actual script, the story line and the dialogue). Meehan was delighted, because he'd long aspired to writing a Broadway show. Sitting in Charnin's office a few days later, he was eager to hear Charnin's brainstorm.

"Here's the idea," Charnin grinned, as Meehan sat poised in his chair! "Little Orphan Annie."

Stunned silence. "You've got to be kidding," Meehan said finally. "That's a rotten idea." As someone who'd disliked "L'il Abner" and "You're a Good Man, Charlie Brown," the only two comic-strip musicals he'd ever seen, he had no interest in working on one himself.

Undeterred, Charnin explained that he didn't want to do a comic-strip musical, but a musical based on the characters in the comic strip.

"What had attracted him to *Little Orphan Annie*," Meehan recalled later, "was the richness of the character of Annie herself—the lost, wandering child, brave, indomitable, a mythic figure in the annals of popular American culture, in contrast with the rough-hewn character of Oliver Warbucks—powerful, dynamic, ruthless, the world's richest man."

By the end of a very long afternoon, Charnin had persuaded

Meehan to at least give it a try. He had already called on Charles Strouse, a two-time Tony Award winner and very successful film and television composer, asking him to write the music.

"I thought it was the worst idea I'd ever heard," was how Strouse described his initial reaction. "Martin didn't really convince me when he first approached me about doing the score with him. I told him I wasn't interested in cartoons and I was afraid it would have to be made campy."

Strouse already had a musical based on a comic-strip character under his belt: *Superman*, which had a brief run on Broadway in 1968. "We got wonderful notices, but did not run," he said in an interview. "Nobody was in the mood for it then. We became known as a kids' show. So I was once burned by cartoons.

"In addition to which, when Martin first brought 'Annie' to me, he had this cartoon-y feel about it. His first idea was to do it with Bernadette Peters. The only way I could become interested in it was if it were done very much in the style of *Oliver!* or a Shirley Temple film. But we worked it out. Tom, Martin, and I all had daughters, and we put a great deal of feeling about our kids into it."

The three men set to work. While Strouse and Charnin began building the score, Meehan studied Gray's comic strips and quickly decided that there was very little in them that could be translated to the stage. "Other than the characters of Annie and Warbucks, there was virtually nothing in the strip that was of any use to us if we weren't to do a cartoon-y musical," he wrote later in the New York *Times*.

So Meehan began to construct his own story. He set it in New York City in 1933 "when America was going through the hardest of hard times," and seized on Gray's—and his own—Dickensian tendencies to weave a story about a two-month-old foundling who had been deposited on the doorstep of the New York Municipal Orphanage back in 1922, with half a silver locket and an anonymous note from her parents promising they would come back someday to claim her.

"In the comic strip, Annie was an orphan whose parentage was totally unexplained," Meehan explained. "As the curtain rises, 11 years have passed and Annie's mother and father still haven't come back for her. So, Annie runs away from the orphanage into the Depression-wracked streets of New York in search of her parents. The story of Annie, as I constructed it in the spring of 1972, is the story of a child's *Odyssey*-like quest for her missing father and mother."

In Gray's strip, of course, Annie had accepted her situation as an orphan without question. After the first week when Annie listened outside Miss Asthma's door and learned only that she once had a mother and father, never again did Gray instill her with any curiosity about her past.

Meehan's book filled in that gap. "What we do in *Annie*," he said shortly after the show opened, "is invent the comic strip. The show starts in a real-looking, dark-hued orphanage and gradually acquires a cartoonlike tone. Only at the end does Warbucks appear in his trademark tux and diamond stickpin and Annie in her simple red dress and curly hair. For the first time she utters the celebrated phrase 'Leapin' lizards!' "

Two sturdy fixtures of Gray's comic strip, Punjab and Asp, were eliminated from Meehan's script (as were some 80 other characters along the way). They didn't fit in for two reasons, one esthetic and the other technical.

"We wanted to invest the thing with as much reality as possible," Charnin said. "Anybody who looked like they couldn't legitimately fit in went early. Punjab was this giant with supernatural powers who threw his cape over people and made them disappear. And the Asp was this mysterious embodiment of the Orient. We just couldn't put them on a stage and make anyone believe in them. Besides, we didn't want to make it an adventure story. We wanted to make it a love story between two orphans. Warbucks is as much an orphan in this musical as Annie is. He doesn't find his parents, he finds his child."

While Meehan wrestled with the plot, Strouse and Charnin assembled the first draft of the score. In the process, they wrote a song that became not only the *Annie* anthem, but one of the most endearing and familiar songs of the entire decade: "Tomorrow."

"We worked together very closely on it," Strouse said. "The music I had written earlier in part for an industrial film that I had done. I had always liked it, and always reserved the rights on it. I remember the ending of the song very strongly, how it was written, because I was very inspired. We were just sailing to that 'Tomorrow, tomorrow, I love you, tomorrow, you're always a day away.' I do remember always being very worried that anybody with a discerning ear would call me to task for writing a song that was definitely outside of the Thirties period. This was a song that a little girl was singing during the Depression in a dirty alley somewhere, though it was a song that sounded like it was written in the late Sixties—the harmonies and the leaps in the melody. Fortunately, nobody ever pointed it out.

"It's become the idea of hope that Annie always stood for. Even in the comic strip, she transmitted it clearly. She was never a pessimist. That was the thing that stayed with us when everything else was being changed. We sometimes made the mistake of making her too sweet, when she was a tough girl. That was one of the things we learned."

By the summer of 1973, the book, lyrics, and music were in good enough shape to be trotted in front of producer James Nederlander, who expressed some interest in the project but never found the time to seriously pursue it. Other producers heard it, but they never quite got around to bidding on it, either. *Annie* was an orphan.

"It was a *major* struggle to have anyone accept it on any credible, real level," Charnin said. "Nobody wanted to invest that kind of money—at the time it was maybe $750,000 to $1 million—in something that they really didn't think would have a chance."

The project was shelved. Meehan packed his book into a cardboard box and put it up in his attic. At about that time, the Tribune syndicate packed it in on the various attempts to keep *Little Orphan Annie* going and put the strip into reruns. Contrary to the song Charnin, Meehan, and Strouse had been singing to anyone and everyone who would listen, it looked like there would be no "Tomorrow" for Annie.

Charnin kept going back to the syndicate every six months to renew his option. He renewed it seven times in all, each time talking faster and harder to convince the syndicate managers that *Annie* would someday be a Broadway musical that would make them a lot of money. Bob Reed was a believer, but it was becoming more and more difficult to justify Charnin's hold on the rights. There were other parties interested in the property.

"Bob Reed, God love him, was one of the most reasonable men I've ever met, and he really wanted it to happen," Charnin remembered with a chill. "But it was more than the danger zone. We were lying on the railroad tracks with the train coming at us."

Annie had been in plenty of jams before. This one was tight, for sure, but she could always count on *someone* to come to her rescue. He did. His name was Michael Price, the executive producer of the Goodspeed Opera House in East Haddam, Connecticut. He listened to *Annie*, liked it, and offered to produce it at Goodspeed.

But Price's offer had its price: he did not want Charnin as director. Charnin insisted. For a solid year, neither man would give in. Finally, Charnin agreed to relinquish the director's chair, but only if he could approve the selection of his successor.

"It was a very tough thing for him to do," Strouse recalled. "We went through a dozen directors who had concepts of it that we all hated. In the end, Michael had the privilege of selecting Martin to be the director."

"THE WORST IDEA I'D EVER HEARD"

Annie was scheduled at Goodspeed for the summer season of 1976, along with two revivals.

The Goodspeed Opera House is a ginger-cake Victorian structure on the Connecticut River some 20 miles south of Hartford. It is a lovely, but very small, regional theater where such very successful musicals as *Man of La Mancha* and *Shenandoah* had first gotten started. It might as well have been Radio City Music Hall as far as Charnin, Meehan, and Strouse were concerned. It was a chance to put *Annie* on a stage. They were booked in for 11 weeks, and given a budget something under $100,000—cigarette change, by Broadway standards, but real money to hire a real cast and make *Annie* a real show.

Some 600 actors responded to the casting call. The role of Oliver Warbucks was given to veteran actor Reid Shelton, a man with numerous stage, television, and motion picture credits—and, for the time being at least, a full head of graying hair. Sandy Faison, a graduate of Chicago's Second City comedy troupe and an actress with many stage and television credits, landed the part of Warbucks' secretary Grace Farrell after auditioning six times in six different outfits, using six different accents. Robert Fitch had Broadway credentials as long as his arm—he'd appeared in 17 shows—and was an accomplished magician; he got the part of the no-good Rooster Hannigan. Veteran stage and television actor Raymond Thorne would be Franklin Delano Roosevelt, distinctive accent and all, and Maggie Task was cast as Miss Asthma. (Her name would later be changed to "Miss Hannigan.")

The script called for three other orphans besides Annie. Four were cast (one as an understudy): Diana Barrows, Danielle Brisebois, Janine Ruane, and Andrea McArdle.

Annie was to be played by 13-year-old Kristen Vigard, described by Charnin as "small, vulnerable, with a beautiful face and natural red hair."

When the company left New York for Goodspeed it had six children and 17 adults in the cast. No dog. Latching onto a trained dog to play Sandy should have been a simple task, but it turned out to be the most difficult. The search was on as soon as the *Annie* company arrived in Connecticut, and ended three weeks later when Bill Berloni, a carpenter and sometime actor on the Goodspeed staff, found a two-year-old mutt, part Airedale, part Irish wolfhound, at the Humane Society in nearby Newington, Connecticut. Berloni paid the eight dollars' bail money and brought the dog to Goodspeed. After a bath, a haircut, and a manicure, he still didn't look very much like Harold Gray's Sandy, but was given the name—and the part—anyway.

There were less than three weeks to opening night, and the cast plunged into frantic rehearsals while the crew constructed and assembled the sets. The script was changed, the music was changed, the lyrics were changed. Finally it was ready—because the calendar said it had to be ready. During the first public performance on the night before the show officially opened, a hurricane struck the area, knocking out the air conditioning and all but one stage light. The audience left. The show went on for five and a half hours. The next night, opening night, it was down to three and a half hours, which was still far too long. It kept shrinking night after night until it reached an acceptable length. The critics from the Connecticut papers came and wrote generally favorabie reviews.

Soon after opening night, Charnin, Meehan, and Strouse came reluctantly to the conclusion that a major change had to be made in the cast. They fired Annie.

Kristen Vigard, they decided, was too nice. She wasn't putting across the tough edge and street smarts that were such crucial elements of Annie's character. She was replaced in the title role by Andrea McArdle.

"It was hard for us to do, and of course hard for her to accept," Strouse said. "We were all very, very guilty about doing it. It was very hard on her. Martin was particularly good, very thoughtful in the way he told her. But nevertheless she had to be told. Kristen was, and is, a very beautiful and gifted performer. But there was a built-in sweetness to her. It was making the show a little too saccharine. The audiences were buying it, but they were a little diabetic over it. It occurred to us that the tough girl, Andrea, would give it that New York tough thing, and we wouldn't be asking the audience for sympathy. That attitude, once we put Andrea in, then permeated Tom's writing to a much greater extent. She stood up to Warbucks, and the whole show became sassier."

Kristen left the show entirely, but was later signed on again to understudy Andrea when the show went to Broadway. She later appeared in another Broadway musical, *I Remember Mama*, and went on to a successful television acting career.

The dilemma of Warbucks was a horse of a different color, having nothing to do with Shelton's acting. There was a schizophrenia built into the part, and it was causing problems.

The creators of *Annie* couldn't get into the right-wing politics that Gray had instilled in Warbucks, but neither could they wean themselves entirely of Gray's view. So they ended with two Daddy Warbucks onstage. And as New York *Times* critic Walter Kerr was about to point out to them, they couldn't have it both ways.

Kerr was one of several New York critics who'd over the years gotten in the habit of making the rounds of the regional theaters, sniffing around for shows that might later turn up on Broadway. He was invited to see *Annie*, and did so at the end of August. Warbucks was still wandering around on stage, wondering in front of everyone if he should remain a rigid capitalist or go shake hands with FDR. Walter Kerr didn't know, either, and said so in a negative review printed in the Sunday *Times* in early September.

In the theater, getting a bad notice from a critic who writes for the New York *Times* is like Superman getting kryptonite for Christmas. Kerr's review of Annie, however, was more like castor oil: it tasted awful, but once you swallowed it, you began to feel much better. Martin Charnin has expressed his gratitude many times since then for that pan.

"I consider the Kerr review tantamount to being the only reason you and I are sitting here talking now," he told an interviewer exactly five years later, after *Annie* had become successful beyond his wildest dreams. "If Kerr had not come up and said what he said, we would not have gotten our act together. He forced us to do a long, hard investigation of the material. At that time we were still straddling ideological lines. We had not squared away Warbucks' relationship to FDR. We had not squared away Warbucks' motives in the world. He was still this munitions manufacturer. It was very difficult for the audience to accept someone who got money from bullets as anybody who had a heart. Kerr's review said we did not make a commitment one way or the other. And you're not funny, he also said."

Counterbalancing the Kerr review was the reaction of the audiences that were seeing *Annie* night after night. They were laughing and crying in the right places, and they began to stand up during the curtain calls.

Enter Mike Nichols and Lewis Allen. Both men were solidly successful in many aspects of show business. Lewis had produced Broadway shows before, but neither of them had seen a show like *Annie* before.

Lewis Allen's wife, writer Jay Presson Allen, was a close friend of Strouse's. After the Allens saw—and loved—*Annie*, they dragged a reluctant Mike Nichols to see it, too. Browbeaten into a seat at the Goodspeed, Nichols sat through a performance and met afterward with Charnin, Meehan, and Strouse. To their astonishment, he told them that not only were they sitting on top of a gold mine, but that he would like to co-produce it with Lewis Allen on Broadway.

Sam Cohn, Nichols and Allen's agent, got the job of raising the million or so dollars it would take to mount *Annie* on Broadway. The money came from a number of sources. One of them was producer

James Nederlander (who finally found the time to get involved with the show); his ownership of the Alvin Theater on West 52nd Street guaranteed *Annie* a home on Broadway. Another was Roger Stevens, head of the Kennedy Center in Washington, D.C., which gave the show a place for a tryout.

One party who turned down the opportunity to participate in *Annie* was Universal Pictures, which, for a $100,000 stake, could have obtained the motion picture rights to the show and did not. Another was the ABC television network, which a couple of years earlier had had the opportunity to buy *Annie* for a Christmas special for $65,000 and turned it down.

Only weeks before, it had looked like the end of the line. "There was a hopelessness hanging around the project," Charnin said of those final weeks in Connecticut. "We were closing at the end of the Goodspeed run and it did not look like anybody was going to pick it up. It would have died a-borning, the company would have been dismantled, and after that happened it would have been relatively impossible to get it back together again."

Instead, everybody packed up and headed back for New York, not as a defeated army, but as a triumphant caravan marching forward to what they believed (or hoped) would be ultimate victory. The show was revised and rehearsed, beginning in mid-January. About 85 percent of it survived all the way from Goodspeed to Broadway.

There was another major cast change: veteran Broadway actress Dorothy Loudon was given the role of Miss Hannigan. Walter Kerr had said the show lacked humor, and the three creators agreed. As she was played at Goodspeed, Miss Hannigan was without laughs; she was a thoroughly diabolical, mirthless villain. The part was rewritten to give her a much more comic personality, and Loudon won it hands down with a hilarious audition performance.

The characterization of Oliver Warbucks was finally straightened out. "We chose to make Warbucks a patriot," Charnin explained. "Warbucks sacrificed everything for this little kid. And if that sacrifice meant collaborating with his enemy—and his greatest enemy could only be FDR—that is the grand gesture that Warbucks would make. Politics and orphans make strange bedfellows. For him to have done any of these things with smaller men would have been beneath Warbucks."

David Mitchell was hired to design the scenery, Theoni V. Aldredge to design the costumes, and Peter Gennaro to design the dance numbers.

Sandy went back to school to learn the six tricks he had to perform during the course of the show. And he was given an understudy, named Arf. Reid Shelton finally shaved his head.

"THE WORST IDEA I'D EVER HEARD"

David Powers was hired to be the show's press agent. He had just come off a million-dollar flop called *Hellzapoppin*, which had closed in Boston. Powers would remember for a very long time afterward that the biggest disaster of his career came just before the biggest success.

As the company was packing for the move down to Washington for a five-week tryout before, it was hoped, returning to open on Broadway, *Annie* was invited to the White House. Jimmy Carter had just been inaugurated as the 39th President of the United States, and he and Rosalynn Carter were hosting a dinner at the White House for the governors of all the states and territories on the evening of March 1. The White House Social Secretary, Gretchen Poston, had flown up to New York to see *Annie* in rehearsal and asked for an abbreviated version of it at the Carters' dinner. March 1 was also the first night of previews at the Eisenhower Theater at the Kennedy Center. After the curtain fell on the show's first full-fledged—and well-received— performance, the entire company was driven to the White House, where the President himself led the standing ovation.

The reaction of the Washington critics on opening night at the Eisenhower was no less enthusiastic. The reviews were the kind that producers write in their dreams—the kind, as Charnin remarked, "that mothers write for their children." Within two and a half days, the entire five-week Washington run was sold out. "The demand was unprecedented for a play, said a Kennedy Center spokesperson," the Washington *Post* reported. "The Center's instant charge telephone system, which can handle 300 calls an hour, was said to be so overburdened yesterday that it broke down three times."

Meg Greenfield, writing in *Newsweek*, noted that if for no other reason, *Annie* was a remarkable achievement in those Watergate-hangover days because "it is a play in which J. Edgar Hoover is a good guy."

"*Annie* gangs up on you, and you experience the most unexpected sentiments: reassurance, a feeling of well-being, and an agreeable connection with a long-gone world—a life built on assumptions and simplicities you had forgotten about," Greenfield wrote. "*Annie* is a kind of one-shot, middle-class, middle-aged trip home." In those euphoric early days of Jimmy Carter's ascendancy, the nation's capital was a haven of optimism where the spirit of *Annie* fit right in. The orphans, particularly Andrea McArdle, were the toast of the capital. Their favorite drink, an Orphan Annie (orange juice and grenadine), took its place at D.C. watering holes alongside martinis and mint juleps.

The mood of a victory dinner after the opening was dampened considerably when, according to Meehan, Nichols raised his glass, toasted the success of the show, and announced: "If we take *Annie* to New York just as it is now, it's going to be one of the biggest flops in Broadway history. You three"—he pointed to Charnin, Meehan, and Strouse—"have got your work cut out for you during the next five weeks."

"We went over *Annie* line by line, note by musical note," Meehan recalled. "By the time it ended its run in Washington, it had lost 20 minutes and gained two musical numbers, replacing three that had been cut."

In that peculiar combination of snobbery and provinciality, New Yorkers in general—and Manhattanites in particular—tend to regard everything that doesn't originate between the Hudson and East rivers as either substandard or overrated. Broadway theatergoers take special delight in looking down their noses at any show that has gotten rave reviews in one of the three other American cities that claim to be centers of culture: Boston, Los Angeles, and Washington.

The wild acclaim *Annie* had received in Washington made it a perfect candidate for stifled yawns, condescending glances, and smug sighs from a typical New York preview audience. But *Annie* was not to be denied. She won them over. She mowed them down. By opening night, newspapers, magazines, and television were swarming all over the Alvin Theater.

The final verdict, however, belonged to the critics, specifically the theater reviewers for the three daily newspapers: Clive Barnes of the New York *Times*, Douglas Watt of the *Daily News*, and Martin Gottfried of the *Post*. Watt had reservations. Gottfried loved it, calling it "a delightful new old-fashioned show" that "deals in out-and-out greasepaint sentiment." The opening paragraph of Barnes' review in the *Times* was sweet salve for the lashing the paper had printed only six months before: "To dislike the new musical *Annie*, which opened last night at the Alvin Theater," Barnes wrote, "would be tantamount to disliking motherhood, peanut butter, friendly mongrel dogs, and nostalgia. It would also be unnecessary, for *Annie* is an intensely likable musical. You might even call it lovable; it seduced one, and should settle down to being a sizable hit."

Kerr himself repented publicly in his review of opening night, which appeared in the *Times* two weeks later. It was excerpted for the theater listings that ran every Sunday in the paper's Arts and Leisure Guide: "An old legend is made into a new one. . . . We're forthrightly invited to lose our minds at the Alvin, and that—reluctantly at first, then helplessly—is what we do."

The reviews were nearly unanimous in their praise and enthusiasm. People lined up in droves outside the Alvin's box office. Ticket orders poured in by phone and mail.

Martin Charnin, Thomas Meehan, and Charles Strouse were delighted. So were Mike Nichols and Lewis Allen and James Nederlander and Roger Stevens. So was everyone in the cast and crew—it meant steady paychecks for everyone, for a long, long time. Bob Reed of the Tribune syndicate was vindicated.

Two months after it opened, *Annie* was nominated for 10 Tonys and won seven: Best Musical, Best Actress in a Musical (Dorothy Loudon), Best Book of a Musical (Thomas Meehan), Best Score of a Musical (Charles Strouse and Martin Charnin), Best Choreography (Peter Gennaro), Best Scenic Designer (David Mitchell), and Best Costumes (Theoni V. Aldredge).

That wasn't all. *Annie* was named Best Musical of the 1976–77 season by the New York Drama Critics Circle. It won five awards from the Outer Critics Circle, seven Drama Desk awards, and Andrea McArdle won a Theatre World Award for most promising new personality on Broadway.

A few wet blankets were to be expected, and they showed up right on schedule. In an article in *New York* magazine that bore the shrieking headline: "Leapin' Lizards! Has Annie Gone Pinko?!?" writer Bob Abel asserted that there was "a very serious ideological question at issue" in the show. Anyone who had followed Annie's adventures in Gray's comic strip over the years, Abel declared, "will have to confront the sight and sound of Daddy Warbucks, the apotheosis of right-wing conservatism in the comics, and Annie, his adoring earpiece, as bloody bleeding-heart liberals, can you believe it!"

Purists, he pointed out, would not recognize the Warbucks who appeared nightly on stage, first cavorting with Roosevelt, then actually planting the idea of the New Deal in the President's brain, and finally—sheer outrage—staying home to take care of Annie. "Meaning no disrespect for the dead," Abel wrote, "but Harold Gray would be calling upon Punjab and the Asp to wreak havoc on Mike Nichols' head, and on those of all others concerned, if he knew what had happened to his favorite people."

If anyone heeded that warning, they could not be found in the line that was by then a constant fixture outside the Alvin.

Like any youngster who's loved and well-fed, *Annie* grew.

It became much more than a Broadway show. It became a phenomenon. The cast album, recorded a week after the show opened, eventually attained the record industry's coveted "platinum" status by virtue of having sold more than a million copies. There were *Annie* T-shirts, *Annie* dolls, *Annie* jewelry, and souvenir books, towels, and fashion clothing for girls. (All of which foreshadowed the much greater merchandising campaign that would surround the movie of *Annie* in 1982.) Nederlander took down the ALVIN sign that had hung outside the theater for 50 years and replaced it with one that read ANNIE. (In 1981, he evicted *Annie* from the Alvin to make way for a short-lived musical. Drifting from theater to theater like the homeless child it portrayed, *Annie* nonetheless continued to do a very strong business.)

The girls who played the orphans—and their less visible mothers—became regulars around Times Square. Andrea became a pinball wizard at a nearby amusement parlor. For all the attention paid to them, the girls seemed remarkably unimpressed with themselves.

Celebrities regularly trouped backstage after each performance. Barbra Streisand shook Sandy's paw, Jacqueline Kennedy congratulated Ray Thorne for his portrayal of FDR, and Muhammad Ali sparred with Andrea for photographers.

Sandy was invited to every party in town and his "pawtograph" was much sought after. Andrea had to hire a secretary to help open her fan mail, which included love letters and proposals of marriage. Press agent Powers had to cope with an unbelievable demand for house seats. "I get calls for tickets from honeymooners, from people having anniversaries, people named Annie, people who are hard of hearing or partially blind," he said. "One man wanted to bring his wife 'because she has only three months to live.' "

By the end of 1977, tickets had been printed through the end of the following year, the show had a $2 million advance, and plans were being made for *Annie* to open in London.

Andrea was 13 when she landed the role of Annie and took it to stardom. She turned 14 later that year and was rapidly being transformed from a girl into a woman. It was a fact of life the show would always face: the trouble with little girls is that they always grow up. It was decided that Andrea would open *Annie* in London and then retire from the show.

She was the only American in the cast. Warbucks was played by Strafford Johns, Sheila Hancock was Miss Hannigan, and seven-year-old Claire Hood, who played one of the orphans, nearly walked away with the show.

It opened in the West End at the Victoria Palace on May 3, 1978, to reviews similar in tone to the ones it had received in New York the previous spring. The *Times* called it "as true a piece of storytelling as has reached our musical stage for many a day . . . a great night out."

"THE WORST IDEA I'D EVER HEARD"

The staid Manchester *Guardian* said "the secret of this show's un-equivocal success is that it artfully waits until the last reel before tampering with tear ducts." The *Evening Standard* called it "an adroit, enchanting musical that shamelessly exploits our weakness for orphans, little girls, and dogs."

The *Daily Mail* lost its cool altogether: "*Annie*, the all-American Broadway musical, barnstormed that citadel of English musical, the Victoria Palace, last night, selling the irresistible opiate for optimism and apple-pie good cheer. I cannot remember when a first-night audience enjoyed itself so hugely. We almost hugged ourselves with delight as *Annie* went arrow-straight to where it aimed: the heart."

Annie went on to play in Tokyo, Mexico City, Johannesburg, Dublin, Stockholm, Melbourne, Sydney, Perth, Manila, Caracas, and other cities all over the world. In September 1979, it made history by becoming the first Broadway musical ever to have four productions playing simultaneously in the United States. The four road companies of *Annie* visited every major city in the U.S. several times over.

Annie paid off its investors within months of its opening on Broadway—an unprecedented feat in a notoriously risky business. The play alone and its assorted touring companies took in more than $100 million in its first four years.

How to explain it? As the critics said, it was a show blessed with a good script, good music, good lyrics, good technical aspects, and very good performances. But it had something else, something not quite tangible, that kept people coming back time and time again.

Writing for the New York *Times* on the fourth anniversary of the show's Broadway opening, Meehan said: "I suspect that it is because *Annie* is an old-fashioned and upbeat retelling of the Cinderella story with a subtext of contemporary social and political comment, and so has elements in it that seem to appeal to just about everyone, from the very young to the very old, from relatively naive teenagers to hard-bitten sophisticates."

For Charnin, the realization would come that the feelings he and the others experienced from *Annie* would never be duplicated: "The constant joy is that I see kids being affected by it. We have little girls all over this country, probably all over the world, who have seen the show and want to be in it, who have learned the songs. It has had an extraordinary effect. We have auditions where 600 kids will come and sit down and open their mouths and sing 'Tomorrow.' I don't think any other show can boast that. I get résumés sent to me by actors constantly. In the last year I've started to get some extraordinary photographs of these gorgeous young ladies who look vaguely familiar. And when I turn them over, I discover that they are the original orphans in some of those companies from all over the world, who are now 15 and 16 and 17 and going on into the world."

Andrea was replaced in the role of Annie on Broadway in February 1978 by her understudy, Shelley Bruce, who was in turn replaced by *her* understudy, Sarah Jessica Parker, in March 1979. The girl who would be the longest-running Annie, Allison Smith, assumed the role in January 1980.

"There will always be a little girl singing 'Tomorrow' somewhere," Charnin said. "The sun will never set. It really won't."

Chapter 9

STARR-ING ANNIE

Little Orphan Annie wasn't the only fading star in the Tribune syndicate's sky as the Seventies wore on. *On Stage*, another veteran comic strip, which had offered an inside look at the world of show business since 1956, was slipping steadily down the subscription list. By 1979, the dwindling income from *On Stage* was causing concern to the syndicate and to its creator, Leonard Starr.

Starr, a former advertising and magazine illustrator, had served an apprenticeship ghost-drawing other comic strips before launching his own. The story of struggling young actress Mary Perkins, trying to make it in the tough world of show business, was familiar ground for Starr. He'd spent many hours as an illustrator drawing models, many of them small-town girls with big ambitions who'd pass the time by telling him their own stories of trying to get a break.

On Stage enjoyed a large and loyal following over the years, and Starr thoroughly enjoyed drawing Mary's long quest for fame and fortune. He won many awards for his vivid, realistic drawing style. Starr took particular pride in his detailed, authentic backgrounds. He spent an enormous amount of time researching the locales where he set *On Stage*, right down to the actual façades of the various Broadway theaters.

It was just that devotion to detail and craftsmanship, however, that was the ultimate undoing of *On Stage*. In the early Seventies, the price of newsprint went up enormously. Shortly afterward, the first

Arab oil boycott sent the price of ink skyrocketing. Those two factors created a cost crunch for all newspapers, and the unfortunate solution to the problem was a general reduction of space. Everything in the papers—advertising, news stories, and features—were tightened up. On the comic pages, the strips were reduced in size in order to fit more of them onto a page.

It was a harsh blow for Starr, who watched as his carefully manicured renderings became so small that the backgrounds were almost impossible to see. It was like looking at the Mona Lisa from across the street. Starr was forced to compensate by drawing the main characters and dialogue larger, and devoting less attention to details. It became an increasingly frustrating exercise. Unlike some of his colleagues, Starr refused to compromise entirely, stubbornly drawing the strip with as much detail as he could.

It was a losing battle, and by the middle of 1979 he was working on another project, a series of adventure comic books for the ravenous European market, while preparing to abandon *On Stage*.

Changes were being contemplated at the syndicate office, too. Ever since *Annie* had become a hit on Broadway two years earlier, both Bob Reed and the syndicate's editor, Don Michel, had been trying to figure out how to revive it as a comic strip. In light of the disastrous earlier efforts, they were proceeding with caution. They saw many samples from artists and writers, but had rejected them all.

They, too, had watched with dismay as the subscriptions to *On Stage* dwindled down. It seemed only a matter of time before it would be retired. Which was a shame, because Starr was one of the few cartoonists around who could both write and draw a continuity strip, and do a consistently good job of it. They got an idea, and Starr got a phone call from Bob Reed. Would he take a crack at *Annie*?

"It did seem a shame," Starr recalled, "since Annie was still very much with us, not to have it in its original form. They couldn't get Harold Gray to do it, but they did want an experienced hand on it. The terms were very good, so I thought I'd give it a whack."

Reed asked Starr to work up three weeks' worth of material. As is his habit, Starr began at the public library in the town where he lived, Westport, Connecticut. Annie would be right at home. Like Gray, Starr was a diligent researcher.

"If you want a perfect world, hand it over to the librarians," Starr is fond of saying. "Librarians will do anything in the world for you." Those guardians of civilizations are especially invaluable to someone working on a dramatic plot, he said: "It's out of research that the cliffhangers come."

For his first sequence, Starr selected the energy crisis. He'd already decided that he would imitate Gray in taking his themes from the headlines of the day. Nothing could have been more contemporary at that time than the energy crisis. Americans were waiting in long lines at gas stations, turning down thermostats, bundling up in wool, and grumbling endlessly about the greedy Arabs who'd jacked up the price of oil.

Enter Daddy Warbucks and his "Lazarus Process" for revitalizing depleted American oilfields. "I haven't been idle," Daddy remarked casually to Annie in Starr's opening panels. "I've *solved* the energy crisis!"

"Leapin' lizards!" she replied.

Shades of eonite! The "Lazarus Process" was cheap, nonpolluting, and could turn abandoned oil wells back into gushers. "By producing ten million or so barrels of oil a day for forty or fifty years—right *here* in this *country*," Daddy explained to Annie, "we can be self-sufficient in energy until we've developed alternate sources." Alas, such a simple and obvious solution to the energy crisis could not, in the Gray tradition, have existed without a healthy measure of government bungling.

"I offered the process to the government—free—several months ago," Daddy remarked.

"You *did*?" Annie said. "Boy! I'll bet *that* made 'em happy!"

"Hard to say," Daddy replied, flicking his cigar. "I haven't received a *reply* to my offer. They've kept me on 'hold,' haven't returned my calls. The key people in the energy bureau have *obviously* made themselves unavailable to me."

"Well, that beats all!" Annie said angrily. "Don't those guys know the shape th' country's in because of *oil*?"

"Strange . . . isn't it, Annie?"

Right off the bat, Starr wanted to invoke the flavor of Gray's best period, the Thirties, in his plot, drawing, and dialogue, and take an important contemporary situation and place Annie right in the middle of it. That was accomplished in short order when Annie was kidnapped by Sheik Bahd-Simel, a desert prince who had the misfortune of being the only ruler in the Middle East whose wind-blown sand doesn't have any oil beneath it. He thought Daddy would hand over the secret of the Lazarus Process in exchange for Annie, safe and sound. Readers of *Little Orphan Annie* over the years knew better than that, of course.

Annie made its first appearance in some 100 newspapers—including the New York *Daily News*—on Sunday, December 9, 1979. The strip featured the logo from the Broadway show.

"If stern traditionalists are disturbed by the word 'new' in 'Annie,' they too can rest easy," wrote Worth Gatewood in a gleeful retraction of the obituary for the strip he'd composed two years earlier. "Annie and Daddy haven't changed a bit. She still has those double-zero eyes, dust-mop hairdo, and that little red dress. He's still in black tie and wing collar, pigeon's egg diamond glittering on his shirtfront. They're still up against as villainous a set of adversaries as ever came out of an inkpot. Annie and Daddy will triumph, of course, as they have for the last 55 years. And even if they didn't, Daddy could always buy Saudi Arabia. Arf!"

In a very short time, the number of papers subscribing to the new strip doubled the number that had been taking the *Little Orphan Annie* reruns. Starr attributed a large part of its success to the freedom he had to pattern his drawings after Gray's best years.

"Hitting on the Thirties style was the best move," Starr said in an interview. "That was the style that struck me as the most charming, where Annie looked the cutest to me. The mistake the other guys made was to imitate Gray's latest stuff, from the Sixties. She didn't look nearly as good then. He'd taken to putting pupils in her eyes occasionally, and she acquired these extra lines around her eyes and around her hair. It sometimes made her look as if she had palsy.

"In the first two or three weeks," Starr went on, "I traced Harold Gray's stuff, just to get the style in my fingers. I'm as faithful to Harold Gray as I can possibly be. You can't imitate him totally. What you have to do is capture the soul of the thing. Early on, I was drawing much the way he would have, but ultimately I thought it was unfaithful to him because people carry a memory of Annie in their minds. They don't remember bad drawing or bad composition, which Gray had from time to time. Annie *lives* for them. If I drew it exactly the way Gray did it, I think they would accuse me of cheapening it. So I do it the best I can, and as faithfully to Harold Gray's style and feeling as possible."

The similarities in plot between *On Stage* (struggling young actress in the treacherous world of show business) and *Annie* (one little girl against the world) made Starr's transition a smooth one. Many editors didn't realize the reruns had been replaced by a brand new set of strips until several weeks after it began. By then, the new *Annie* was an established success. Within two years, it was once again one of the most popular comic strips in the country, appearing in some 400 North American newspapers.

"Gray had three strong themes," Starr said. "One was Dickensian: the orphan and depressed times. He must have been a real Dickens aficionado, which I happen to be as well. He had his Macawbers and

Pecksniffs. Dickens was actually a cartoonist, you know. His characters were all larger than life, and they are very caricatured. So you can see why a cartoonist would be very big on him. All his characters were beautifully drawn and developed, but all sorts of exaggerated, which is the essence of cartooning, really.

"And then Gray had a political thing. He was very conservative, of course, and maintained his ground up until he died. My leanings are conservative, but not to quite that degree. My voting record is about evenly divided between Democrats and Republicans. I am very big on free enterprise. A quick look at the world will indicate that the free-enterprise system gave America the highest standard of living for more people than anyone in the entire history of the world.

"Gray's third theme was fantasy. I'm not big on fantasy and whimsy. I do some of it, but it's not my favorite thing to do."

Starr decided to key the strip to current events. "My Annie, Sandy, Daddy Warbucks, Punjab, the Asp, and their friends and enemies are involved in issues that affect us all—such things that affect our lives. I do want to offer a personal point of view. I think people want a strip that says something. Gray's Annie did, and mine will, too.

"One of the terrible things is doing the research on it," Starr said. "I really don't know what's going on with all this stuff until I research it." Starr's research has led him into such areas as medical fraud, corruption on Capitol Hill, and the ecology movement.

"The key thing is to not get carried away with research," he continued. "The danger with research is that you begin to lecture people. The last thing on earth the reader wants is to be educated. I used to do very complete outlines, but I found that I digressed from them. So now I'll just get a general sense of the story and where it's gonna go. If I have my punchline, then I'll make it. Sometimes, if nothing has come up, I'll start with a premise and deliberately paint myself into a corner. I figure that if *I* don't know how to get out of it, the reader will be hanging on the same way. Some of the best stories come up that way."

Starr is the first one to admit that the strip's success has more to do with the scenario created by Harold Gray than anything else. "Gray really did give us a terrific cast. Daddy is as much of a character as there ever has been in American fiction. Despite his decidedly capitalistic leanings, he's not the kind of guy to hang around the boardroom. He goes right out there in the field."

But the central character and single most important element in the strip remains Annie. Starr's Annie was the same age as Gray's—about 11.

One thing Starr has changed about Annie was to update her sexual morality a bit. Soon after he began drawing *Annie*, Starr gave her a boyfriend, a pageboy in Congress. Gray hardly ever let anyone make a pass at his Annie, and when they did, she usually responded with that famous fast left. All kisses and hugs were reserved for either Sandy or Daddy. Starr's Annie once found herself cornered in the middle of the night in the Capitol building by gun-wielding crooks. Her only companion was the pageboy, Huckie Flynn, who suggested slyly that they might stay warmer if they put their arms around each other.

"Aw, grow up!" Annie told him.

"That's what I'm *trying* to do!" he replied.

"She's right at the age," Starr said. "These days, they start dating at 11 or 12. They're going to the movies and parties. But we certainly won't get into any heavy necking or anything."

Annie's wardrobe, too, was updated. "I was drawing it, and I suddenly realized that I haven't seen a little girl in a dress in ages. I put her in a dress as often as I can, but if she's off on a ship or on an island running around in a little red dress it looks funny."

Two other aspects of the original strip have been preserved by Starr: the Sunday homily ("It can take me as long to find the quote as it does to do the whole Sunday story") and the use of personification in naming his characters ("May Flowers" was Daddy's girlfriend, "Anya Toze" the ballet instructor, "Huckie Flynn" the Capitol pageboy, "Senator Brassie" the young Senator, "Dr. Bunsen" the scientist).

"The names are hard to come by," Starr said. "Gray got very lazy with his names toward the end. I try to be a little sharper with them."

One aspect of Gray's style, however, would never be changed by Leonard Starr. "I wouldn't fool around with pupils," he swore solemnly.

Chapter 10

ANNIE:
THE MOVIE

Christmas came early for Messrs. Charnin, Meehan, and Strouse in 1977. As their red-headed protégée might have said, it was the swellest one ever. After many months of negotiations, they signed a contract in mid-December with Columbia Pictures, giving that studio the rights to make *Annie* into a movie for the staggering sum of nearly $10 million.

The amount literally took everyone's breath away. "We were, if nothing else, the deal that stopped the deals," Charnin said in retrospect, and predicted: "There will never be a deal like that again."

The exact sum of $9.5 million was nearly double the highest amount previously paid for motion picture rights to a Broadway show.

Why would any studio pay such an enormous sum just to obtain the *right* to make a movie? To it would have to be added all the normal production costs associated with making a movie musical— always an expensive proposition. And there was always the risk that it would bomb at the box office. If *Annie* had flopped on Broadway, its producers and backers would have been out a million bucks. Before the ink was even dry on the contract, Columbia had put itself at risk for ten times as much. The studio, however, was convinced that the property was worth every penny.

At first, the three creators of *Annie* wanted to retain artistic control over the movie. But as the negotiations wore on, it became clear that

Columbia was willing to pay them a substantial amount of money to gain a free hand in making the film. "In the end," Meehan said, "the lawyers and accountants advised us to take the money." They did.

Having secured *Annie*, Columbia assigned David Begelman as its executive producer. Begelman chose as his director Randal Kleiser, who had directed the motion picture version of another hit Broadway musical, *Grease*, which had gone on to become the highest-grossing musical in Hollywood's history.

It was agreed that Meehan would write the screenplay for the film, that Gennaro would be its choreographer, and that Theoni Aldredge would design the costumes. The various roles of *Annie* quickly became the most sought-after parts in the movie business. Agents jockeyed and jostled with each other in the struggle to land their clients one of the plum roles.

But before things had gone too far, Begelman resigned from Columbia. The project was then offered to Ray Stark. A former literary and talent agent, Stark had a long string of successes behind him. He'd hit the big time in 1968 with *Funny Girl*, a musical biography of Fanny Brice (Stark's own mother-in-law), with Barbra Streisand. In 1980, the same year he was given *Annie* to produce, he was presented with the Irving Thalberg Award by the Academy of Motion Picture Arts and Sciences for his lifetime's achievement in films.

Stark made changes. Meehan's screenplay was returned to him; the assignment went instead to screenwriter Carol Sobieski. Gennaro was replaced by British choreographer Arlene Phillips. And Stark hired 75-year-old John Huston to direct *Annie*.

The announcement raised eyebrows in Hollywood and on Broadway. Despite the abundant credits Huston could boast after 50 years of writing, directing, and acting in films, the only experience he had had with musicals was the classic *Moulin Rouge*. His credits included 13 Academy Award nominations, two of which he won, for writing and directing *The Treasure of the Sierra Madre* in 1948. Other famous films that bore his name in the credits included *The Maltese Falcon*, *The African Queen*, *The Asphalt Jungle* and *The Man Who Would Be King*. But was *this* the director who should be behind the lens for *Annie*? Columbia and Ray Stark thought so.

Huston, in a postproduction studio interview, described the story of *Annie* as "very much in the American grain. I hate to use so pompous a phrase as 'American folklore' but I guess it does come under that heading. It's comic-book in origin, and we've attempted to keep it very broad, but pointed and funny."

Direct responsibility for the musical production numbers in the film was handed to the executive producer, Joe Layton, who'd just finished directing the Tony Award-winning musical *Barnum* on Broadway. The most difficult adjustment they would make on *Annie*, he said later, was the amount of time it took to film it. "I'm used to putting a show on the stage, rehearsed and ready to go, in five weeks," he said. "Movies seem like forever."

Theoni Aldredge stayed on as costume designer. And Strouse and Charnin were hired to write four new songs for the movie: "We've Got Annie", "Sign", "Let's Go to the Movies" and "Sandy" (which was later retitled "Dumb Dog").

The search for the girl to play Annie in the movie began in early 1980. Finding little—and not-so-little—girls willing to audition for the plummest child role since the days of Shirley Temple was no problem at all; every stage mother in the Free World had her eye on the part. But finding just the right little girl was a tough task.

The qualifications were stringent. The filmmakers had to face the same set of problems Charnin, Meehan, and Strouse had faced four years earlier: their Annie would have to be able to act, sing, and dance, and had to possess the traits needed to put the orphan girl across. She had to be vulnerable and none too slick to win the hearts of the audience, but she had to be tough, too, to make believable a streetwise orphan who had to fend for herself in a hostile world.

There were other problems, too. The movie would take nearly a year to make; the schedule called for filming to begin in the spring of 1981, with the movie to be released more than a year later. The movie Annie had to be young enough so that there was no danger she would blossom into adolescence before the crucial publicity campaign that would begin shortly before release date. Andrea McArdle had been forced to leave the Broadway show after only one year for precisely that reason. It wouldn't do for the movie Annie to outgrow the part that soon—a teenage girl with a developing figure showing up for the premiere or on the talk shows would not do.

"Annie is a role that requires an enormously gifted child with that special dynamic talent to sing, dance, and act," Stark said at the outset. He enlisted seven former child stars to advise him: Jackie Coogan, Gloria Jean, Jane Withers, Peggy Ann Garner, Donald O'Connor, and Patty Duke Astin. "These former child stars, with their professional backgrounds and own childhood experiences, can be of invaluable assistance to us in discovering our star," Stark said. "They know what it takes."

In June 1980, casting director Garrison True arrived in New York City and installed himself at the Plaza Hotel for the first three weeks of a six-month talent search, the biggest and most publicized since

THE HISTORY OF LITTLE ORPHAN ANNIE

David O. Selznick went looking for Scarlett O'Hara in 1938. True's method was to interview each applicant personally. Those who showed potential were called back and videotaped, and the tapes were sent back to Burbank for Stark, Huston, and Layton to evaluate.

More than 2,000 girls showed up at the Plaza. True later moved on to 22 other cities in his quest for Annie, and beating those other bushes eventually yielded two of the orphans. But unknown to him at the time, he had found his Annie at the Plaza.

Standing in the line that became a fixture around the hotel during True's stay there was a nine-year-old girl from Yardley, Pennsylvania, named Aileen Quinn. When her turn came, she impressed True enough to rate a stint in front of the video camera. Her tape, along with those of other girls, was sent off to Hollywood.

Aileen's mother, a schoolteacher and occasional actress, had brought the youngster along on various community-theater auditions in Pennsylvania. Aileen, who'd been studying ballet and tap dancing since she was five, soon landed roles in regional and stock productions of *The King and I*, *Gypsy*, *Annie Get Your Gun*, and *Carousel*. Then Aileen and Mrs. Quinn headed for New York, where she appeared in three television commercials before auditioning for *Annie*.

(At about the same time, Aileen auditioned for the Broadway production of *Annie*, and was hired as the "swing" orphan—the understudy for all six of the orphans. She had to learn all six roles as well as commute every day from Yardley, two hours each way. She joined the show in July 1980 and left it the following January, when filming on *Annie* started.)

In November 1980, after studying the tapes sent to them by True, Stark, Huston, and Layton narrowed the list of candidates for Annie down to nine girls and invited them to travel to California for further screening. (All nine eventually appeared in the movie.) Over Thanksgiving weekend at the Beverly Hilton, the list was narrowed to three. The trio was asked back again for actual screen-testing with actor Albert Finney, who had already been signed for the role of Daddy Warbucks. Then the decision was made.

On January 14, 1981, a press conference was called in Los Angeles to announce that Aileen would play Annie in the movie. Two other finalists, eight-year-old Angela Lee of Los Angeles, and ten-year-old Robin Ignico of Clearwater, Florida, won roles as orphans.

In short order, the casting of *Annie* was completed:

—*Oliver Warbucks* would be played by Finney—the fifth movie role he'd performed in short succession after a six-year absence from the screen. Nominated for an Academy Award for his performance in the film adaptation of Henry Fielding's lusty novel *Tom Jones*, Finney was well known to audiences as the famed Belgian detective Hercule Poirot in Agatha Christie's *Murder on the Orient Express*, an English factory worker in *Saturday Night and Sunday Morning* and in the title role of *Scrooge*, a musical adaptation of Dickens' "A Christmas Carol."

The prospect of playing the caricatured Daddy Warbucks was in keeping with Finney's penchant for character roles. "It calls for bold, simple colors," he remarked. "And it gives me a chance to sing and tap dance."

—*Miss Hannigan* would be played by veteran comedienne Carol Burnett. The 11-year run of her television series *The Carol Burnett Show* accumulated 18 Emmy Awards. Though she had a host of other stage, screen, and TV roles behind her, Miss Hannigan would be her first in a major movie musical.

—*Grace Farrell* would be played by Broadway dancer Ann Reinking. She had been in a string of hit Broadway musicals: *Coco*, *Cabaret*, *Chicago*, *A Chorus Line* and *Dancin'*. Her previous film appearances were with George C. Scott in *Movie, Movie*, and in Bob Fosse's *All That Jazz*.

—*Rooster Hannigan* would be played by Tim Curry, another English actor who'd started in *The Rocky Horror Show* and portrayed Mozart in Peter Shaffer's *Amadeus*.

—*Punjab* would be played by Geoffrey Holder, about whom a studio biography noted "merely acted and did not exercise his usual array of powers, including doing the choreography, designing the costumes and sets, dancing, directing, writing, composing the music, or cooking, among other things." Holder had won Tony awards both as director and costume designer of *The Wiz* on Broadway.

—*FDR* would be played by Edward Herrman, an actor who'd already played that President twice before, winning an Emmy nomination for *Eleanor and Franklin*, and a Critics Circle Award for its sequel, *The White House Years*.

—*Lily St. Regis* would be played by Bernadette Peters, who was an actress Martin Charnin had in mind several years before, when he'd toyed briefly with the notion of doing *Annie* as a camped-up show. In the meantime, her movie credits had included *The Jerk* and *Pennies from Heaven*.

—*The Asp* would be played by movie newcomer Roger Minami, a dancer who'd just finished a two-year world tour with Liza Minnelli's *The Act*.

—*The Orphans* would be played by six girls, ages six through 13, whose résumés ranged from nursing-home performances to national tours of Broadway shows. The youngest, Toni Ann Gisondi, of Bayonne, New Jersey, was only two years old when *Annie* opened on Broadway, and just five when she auditioned for the role of Molly in the movie. The oldest, Rosanne Sorrentino, was 13, and had auditioned for the movie role of Pepper, the toughest orphan, while in New Orleans with one of the national touring companies of *Annie*. Eleven-year-old Robin Ignico was one of the three finalists for the role of Annie. Instead, she was cast to play Duffy. Lucie Stewart, nine years old, played Molly in the London production of *Annie*, but because of British child labor laws, had to leave the show after three months. She was one of the nine semifinalists for the role of Annie, and was eventually signed to play July. Lara Berk was eight when she won the role of Tessie, the nervous orphan. She'd appeared in an Off Broadway children's musical, *Really Rosie*, and had won the part of Molly in one of the road companies of *Annie*, but had to turn it down because her mother couldn't leave her three-year-old sister at home alone. Kate, the romantic orphan, would be played by 11-year-old April Lerman, also an alumna of *Really Rosie* and one of the touring companies of *Annie*, in which she had played Tessie.

—*Sandy* would be played by a six-year-old Otterhound named Bingo, owned by animal trainer Moe di Sesso; he had three understudies.

Finding the actors was one thing; finding places for them to act was another. The story was set in New York, and the city itself would provide much of the background for filming the movie.

In June 1980, nearly a full year before the first day of filming, production designer Dale Hennessey and location manager Robert Paradiso arrived in Manhattan to begin scouting shooting sites. They quickly decided that Radio City Music Hall, Lincoln Center, the New York Public Library, and Washington Square Park would be used.

The opening sequence called for shots of Sandy roaming along through the city, and places like the Manhattan Bridge, an elevated subway track in Brooklyn, and a Chinatown street were selected for that.

Hennessey and Paradiso then turned to the more difficult chore of finding a mansion to serve as Warbucks' home, a building on which to model an orphanage, and a bridge for the chase scene.

The mansion that was finally selected was the administrative building of Monmouth College in West Long Branch, New Jersey—of which Paradiso was an alumnus. Named Woodrow Wilson Hall, the 130-room building had been erected in 1928 at a cost of more than

$10 million by Hubert Parson, then president of the F.W. Woolworth Company.

The orphanage appearing in *Annie* would not be a real building. Given the extensive amount of exterior and interior shots that would be needed, and the commensurate amount of disruption and chaos that would result if they tried to film it on location in New York, the filmmakers decided to construct a set at the Burbank Studios. It would be a New York City street as it might have looked in the Thirties.

Hennessey found his models for the orphanage in two buildings on the Lower East Side of Manhattan: a four-unit apartment building on Mott Street, and a former Children's Aid Society home, built in the late 19th Century, on Sixth Street and Avenue B. Using hundreds of photographs, both present-day and from the Thirties, Hennessey designed a street set with the orphanage as its centerpiece. So impressed were studio executives with its design that they offered to pay any extra costs if it could be made a permanent set on the Burbank lot. It cost more than $1 million when it was finished, and was the product of the labor of more than 130 carpenters, plasterers, painters, heavy-equipment operators, and general workmen. It measured 270 feet long, 29 feet wide, with four-story building façades 67 feet tall, and was unique in being closed at both ends, allowing cameras to rotate 360 degrees on a continuous shot.

(On July 20, 1981, midway through the shooting of *Annie*, Hennessey died of a heart attack at the age of 54. A month later, the street set that was his last project was dedicated in his memory, and officially named "Dale Hennessey Street.")

Hennessey's "street" had some extraordinary qualities not found on most movie sets. At the time he designed it, Joe Layton and Arlene Phillips hadn't finalized their production numbers, so everything on the street had to be built sturdily so it could be used, if necessary, in the music-and-dance numbers. That included everything down to the 53 fire escapes, Paradiso had bought from a New York contractor who was tearing down some buildings in the Bronx and Manhattan; they were dismantled and trucked out to California. Construction coordinator Gary Martin, sent to San Francisco on an unsuccessful mission to obtain period fire escapes, came back instead with a cast-iron railing from the famous City of Paris department store, which was about to be torn down; it was suitably installed near the orphanage. Paradiso's scrounging expeditions around the New York area yielded traffic signals from the Thirties, and from a salvage yard under the Brooklyn Bridge he got three old fire-alarm boxes, some manhole covers, and an old fireplug that was reproduced sixfold in fiberglass. Additional cornices and moldings to dress up the building came from the studio lots at Burbank, Paramount, and Fox, or were manufactured on the lot.

When it was finished, it was estimated that Hennessey's New York street had consumed enough money, material, and labor to build 20 conventional houses.

Finding the bridge was a mind-bender. Actually, Paradiso *did* find the bridge—the exact bridge that screenwriter Carol Sobieski had described in the climactic scene depicting Annie's flight from Rooster up an open drawbridge, to be rescued by Punjab, dangling from a helicopter. Sobieski's bridge "turned out to be on the edge of a pier and it was perfect," Paradiso told the magazine *On Location*. "There was only one problem. It was on oil-company land and the firm planned to demolish it the next day, which they did."

That meant looking for another bridge—one that had a period look to it, was in New Jersey so the cast and crew wouldn't have to travel too far to get to it, and was no longer used by rail or automobile traffic.

With the help of Steve Gorelick, production coordinator for the New Jersey Motion Picture and Television Commission, Paradiso found an abandoned railroad bridge over the Passaic River that had a 180-foot-high drawbridge section permanently raised at an 80-degree angle.

When Huston and the cast and crew of *Annie* arrived in New York to begin shooting on April 29, 1981, the locations where they would be working were as ready as they would ever be.

Breathing down their necks was the threat of a film directors' strike, which would have halted production indefinitely, destroying the film's timetable for release in the spring of 1982.

After shooting the title sequence and Sandy's solo stroll, they moved into Radio City Music Hall for six days of shooting. The script called for Daddy and Annie to go to a private screening, which included a live musical production number with dancing ushers and usherettes—and, of course, the Rockettes. Since there was nobody in the audience but Daddy and Annie, shooting proceeded smoothly and on schedule.

The *Annie* contingent—150 people packed into 14 trucks and 11 campers—then crossed the Hudson River for the long shooting schedule at the Monmouth College building that would appear on film as Warbucks' Fifth Avenue mansion. The preproduction crew had come there several weeks earlier, in the middle of spring semester, but the college obliged them by vacating the building.

Set decorator Marvin March and his 11-person unit arrived with four big trucks filled with the extensively researched furnishings that would fill the Warbucks home. Everything already there that didn't fit in with the "look" March had decided on would have to be removed. But because the building was listed in the National Register of Historic Places, the structure itself could not be altered. The movie people had to satisfy themselves with the interior of all furniture and fixtures, except wall mountings and ceiling lights, and remodeling the grounds slightly.

Among the furnishings March trucked in were an Aubusson rug measuring 22 feet by 30 feet and valued at $80,000; a number of Oriental vases worth $20,000 apiece; two torches worth $120,000 that were placed at the foot of the grand staircase; Grecian busts of marble; eight Louis XV gilded chairs for the main hall; replicas of Rembrandt's *Night Watch*, *La Giaconda* (the Mona Lisa), and the statue *Winged Victory* that stands at the head of the main staircase in the Louvre; a print box for the library from the Mark Hopkins mansion in San Francisco; a ship's wheel in the library that belonged to Jack L. Warner; two serving carts that had been used in the movie *Hello, Dolly!*; a billiard table on loan from the Guggenheim Museum; a 25-foot dining-room table constructed for the movie, with 24 matching chairs; and draperies for 100 inside windows and 60 outside windows, measuring up to 14 feet high.

"This house just sucks up furniture like a vacuum cleaner," March remarked when he was finished.

Warbucks' limousines had arrived earlier—a 1929 Duesenberg Dual Cowl Phaeton and a 1930 du Pont Royal Town Car, both borrowed from Harrah's Automobile Collection in Reno, Nevada.

Huston and the film company spent six weeks at Monmouth during the course of which he was awarded an honorary Doctor of Humane Letters degree for his "life's work, a distinguished array of film narratives embodying a richly diverse gallery of human questors and their elusive prizes." Among the sequences filmed at Monmouth was the finale, a Fourth of July nighttime celebration, complete with fireworks.

Shooting on the railroad bridge began in early June. The production crew painted over the graffiti that covered the bridge, cleared away thick undergrowth, set up lights on barges, built a heliport for the helicopter from which the scenes would be shot and for the "autocopter" from which Punjab would dangle when he rescued Annie.

The filming began on a hot, humid night with more than 100 crew members present. Bobby Porter, a 29-year-old stunt man, was wearing Annie's famous red dress; he was Aileen Quinn's stunt double for the bridge scenes. Jerry Brutsche, the stunt coordinator for the picture, would stand in for Tim Curry as Rooster. The script called for Porter to scramble up the full 180-foot length of the upraised drawbridge, pursued close behind by Brutsche. Moviegoers would see Annie cornered at the very top by Rooster, only to be lifted away at the last second by Punjab (doubled by stunt man Jophery Brown) while Rooster plummeted down the bridge.

The top of the bridge was being built in replica back in Burbank, where Aileen Quinn, Tim Curry, and Geoffrey Holder would appear on camera.

Night after night, Porter and Brutsche scrambled up and down the bridge, while Brown dangled from the hovering autocopter. When they were finished, Huston and the real cast members arrived for some insert shots on the bridge, the landing of the autocopter with Annie and Punjab safe and sound, and her embrace by a thankful Warbucks.

The last major sequence to be shot on the East Coast was the long run the orphans make up Fifth Avenue from the orphanage to Warbucks' uptown mansion—in reality from Washington Square Park up Fifth Avenue past the New York Public Library, the Plaza Hotel, and other landmarks, all the while hotly pursued by Miss Hannigan.

The shooting had to be done in the middle of the night, since it would have been impossible to block off portions of Fifth Avenue to daytime traffic. As it was, the sequence required the crew to set up at each location, dress up that particular stretch of the avenue to look like the Thirties, shoot the action, and break for the next location. When the last take was finished, Annie broke camp and headed back to Burbank to finish the movie at the studio's sound stages and on Hennessey's street set.

The actual filming of Annie was completed on Friday, September 4, 1981—four months after principal photography began, and four years after the project was originally conceived. It had cost some $35 million, and had required the talents of nearly 2,000 people. The cast and crew said their good-bys and went their respective ways, while the raw film itself passed into the hands of the editors and technicians who would put it into final form.

The world premiere of Annie came in mid-May 1982 in New York, Los Angeles, and Toronto. By June the movie was playing in theaters all over the world. Long before it was released, Columbia's research department reported that Annie enjoyed a public recognition factor nearly as high as McDonald's hamburgers, and confidently predicted that *Annie* would be the most eagerly awaited motion picture in history.

The arrival of *Annie* at local movie houses was not the final chapter of her saga—nothing about her is ever "final"—but it brought to a full circle the adventures that had begun on the comic pages of local newspapers so long ago. *Annie* had all the elements that had held the atttention of millions of people for 58 years. It was a darn good story about an orphan, a stray dog, and the richest man in the world.

THE STORY OF MR. AM

Harold Gray reached the peak of his drawing and story-telling powers in the thirties. This sequence, which appeared in 1937, placed Annie, Sandy, and Daddy in a tropical jungle where they met the mysterious Mr. Am. With his help, Daddy's enemies were once again defeated. Mr. Am has been interpreted variously as God, as Santa Claus, and as an extraterrestrial being. Gray brought him back into the strip about once every decade afterward, and in late 1981 he turned up again in the new comic strip drawn by Leonard Starr.

123

Panel 1:
LEAPIN' LIZARDS! IT'S LIKE SOMETHIN' OUT OF A FAIRY STORY— IS HE BIG! AND THOSE WHISKERS— A LOT LIKE SANTA CLAUS— AND THAT FUNNY BOAT---

Panel 2:
AND ALL THOSE MEN WITH HIM— THEY LOOK LIKE I BET SLAVES MUSTA LOOKED WAY BACK IN TH' "ARABIAN NIGHTS" TIMES—

THOSE, ANNIE, ARE HIS MOST WILLING SLAVES— IT IS A GREAT HONOR TO SERVE SUCH A MASTER—

HAROLD GRAY
4-20-37

Panel 3:
OH, GOODY! I FIGGERED MR. AM WOULD BE ALONG PRETTY SOON— AHOY, MR. AM!

AHOY, ANNIE! DOING A LITTLE FISHING, I SEE—

Panel 4:
WELL, I HAVEN'T BEEN VERY LUCKY SO FAR— GUESS WATCHIN' OUT FOR ALLIGATORS MAKES ME TOO JITTERY—

ALLIGATORS! HO! HARMLESS LIZARDS— YOU SHOULD HAVE BEEN AROUND A FEW MILLION YEARS AGO—

Panel 5:
WHY, I USED TO HAVE TO RUN FOR MY LIFE TO AVOID BEING TRAMPLED BY HERDS OF GIANT BRONTOSAURI, EACH AT LEAST A HUNDRED FEET LONG AND WEIGHING THIRTY TONS OR SO— AND TYRANNOSAURUS REX ---

Panel 6:
WHY, ONE OF THEM WOULD EAT ALLIGATORS SAME AS WE EAT SARDINES— BUT THEY ONLY LASTED ABOUT A HUNDRED MILLION YEARS— THOSE WERE THE EXCITING DAYS—

WHEW!

HAROLD GRAY
4-21-37

124

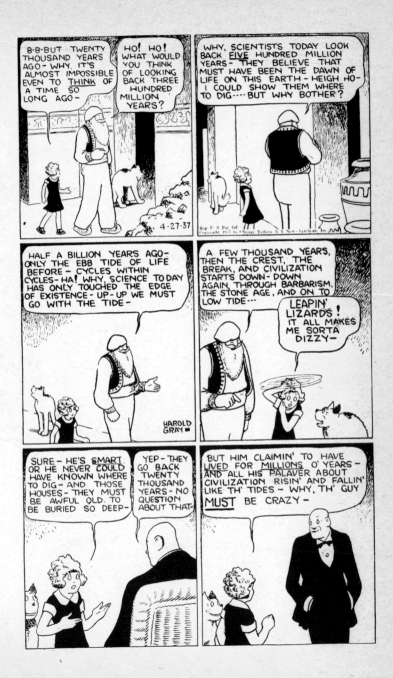

133

135

139

142

143

144

EPILOGUE

This should be the place where a bold and definitive statement appears, something along the line of: "The most remarkable thing about Annie is . . ." It does not.

She's remarkable, all right. But trying to pinpoint all the whys and wherefores is like trying to pick up mercury with your fingers. It can't be done.

Here's the best I could come up with: Annie is the ageless American heroine who's been with us through good times and bad, and there's no reason on earth why she shouldn't go on forever.

The very last words belong to Annie. She said them in 1931: "It's not so much how yuh start out that counts. It's how yuh finish."

INDEX

Abby and Slats (comic strip), 84
ABC (network), 96
Abel, Bob, 99
Adventure Time with Orphan Annie (radio program), 38–40
Alden, Caleb (character), 36–37
Alden, Mrs. (character), 36
Aldredge, Theoni V., 96, 99, 110
Ali, Mohammed, 100
Allen, Jay Presson, 95
Allen, Lewis, 95, 99
Alvin Theater, 96, 98–100
Am, Mr. (character), 121
America (magazine), 71
American Mercury, 47
Andre, Pierre, 40
Annie (character), 68, 69, 75, 80, 84–85, 111–12; age of, 76; character of, 2, 13–14; description of, 6, 76, 84–85, 106–8; during the 30's, 24–25, 42–44; during World War II, 46–51; eyes of, 75–76, 106, 108; Gray on, 56–57, 65; and Junior Commando movement, 46–51; in reruns, 85; Starr on, 103
Annie (film; 1982), 100, 109–19
Annie (musical), 88–102
Annie Fanny (character), 77
Annie Rooney (character), 20–21
Apathy, Al (character), 12
Arf (dog), 96
Arf! The Life and Hard Times of Little Orphan Annie (book), 88
Arnold, Henry, 83
Asp (character), 28, 43, 48, 82, 91, 113
Asthma, Miss (character), 3, 10–11, 16, 20, 91, 93. *See also* Hannigan, Miss.
Astin, Patty Duke, 111
Axel (character), 47, 66

Bahd-Simel, Sheik (character), 105
Bank Holiday (1933), 28–29
Barnes, Clive, 98
Barrows, Diana, 93
Baruck, Allen, 39
Begelman, David, 110
Bell, Shirley, 38, 42, 43
Bergmann, Lyle, 41
Berk, Lara, 114
Berloni, Bill, 93
Bill (character), 26
Bingo, 114
Blaisdell, Philip "Tex," 83–84, 88
Bleating-Hart, Melvin (character), 61
Bleating-Hart, Mrs. J. (character), 60–61

Blondie (comic strip), 83
Bluster, Phil O. (character), 31
Boston *Herald Traveler,* 50
Boston University, 27
Bottle, Mrs., (character), 16
Bottle, "Pop" (character), 16
Bowles, Chester, 53
Brassie, Senator (character), 108
Brice, Fanny, 110
Bridgeport *Herald,* 56–57
Bringing Up Father (comic strip), 83
Brisebois, Danielle, 93
Broun, Heywood, 29
Brown, Jophery, 118
Browning, Dorothy, 14
Browning, Edward West, 14–16
Browning, Nellie, 14
Bruce, Shelley, 102
Brutsche, Jerry, 118
Buffalo *Evening News,* 86
Bullion, Tom (character), 24
Bunsen, Dr. (character), 108
Burnett, Carol, 113

Caplin, Elliott, 84, 88
Capp, Al, 72, 84
Captain Midnight (radio program), 41, 43
Carter, Jimmy, 97
Carter, Rosalynn, 97
Cartoonist ProFiles (magazine), 73
"Cassandra" (pseudonym), 66
Catholic Standard, 70
Chance, Rose (character), 36
Chandler, Norman, 67, 80
Charnin, Martin, 88, 89, 94, 95, 96–102, 109, 111
Chicago Edison Company, 30
Chicago *Tribune,* 7, 9, 13, 17, 35, 46, 54, 65
Chicago Tribune–New York News Syndicate, 13. *See also* Tribune Company Syndicate.
Child labor, 65
Cincinnati *Enquirer,* 79
Claptrap, Claude (character), 33–34
Coates, Paul, 80
Cohn, Sam, 95
Columbia Pictures, 44, 109–10
Comic strips, reader polls of, 79–80
Communism, 64, 67
Coogan, Jackie, 111
Corntassle, Joe (character), 39, 40
Coronet (magazine), 50
Curry, Tim, 113, 118

"Daddy and Peaches" scandal (1926), 14–16

Dahm, Frank, 38–39

Daily Oklahoman, 79

Dallas *Times-Herald*, 78

De Tour, Count (character), 17, 19

Detroit *Free Press*, 66

Di Sesso, Moe, 114

Dickens, Charles, 12, 106

Dick Tracy (comic strip), 80

Doonesbury (comic strip), 57

Dr. Kildare (comic strip), 84

"Dumb Dog" (song), 111

Eaton, Cyrus, 30

Edison, Thomas, 30

Editor & Publisher (magazine), 9, 50, 54

Edmonton (Canada) *Journal*, 70

Edson, Gus, 83

Encyclopedia of Mystery and Detection, The (Steinbrunner), 42–43

Eon, Eli (character), 32, 34

"Eonite," 32–34

Faison, Sandy, 93

Fairfield (Conn.) *News*, 53

Fanny, Annie (character), 77

Farrell, Grace (character), 93, 113

Finney, Albert, 112–13

First National Bank of Westport, 73

Fisher, Bud, 83

Fitch, Robert, 93

Flack, Robert C., 51–56

Flask, Fred (character), 51–56

Flowers, May (character), 108

Flynn, Huckie (character), 108

Ford, Henry, 32, 35

Fritter, Fred (character), 12

Frost, Winifred, 20. *See also* Gray, Winifred Frost.

Garner, Peggy Ann, 111

Gasoline Alley (comic strip), 7, 83

Gatewood, Worth, 86, 106

Gehman, Richard, 39

Gennaro, Peter, 96, 99, 110

George (character), 57

Gilles, Ann, 44

Gisondi, Toni Ann, 114

Gloria Jean, 111

Goodspeed Opera House (East Haddam, Conn.), 92, 93

Gooney, Sweet Fanny (character), 77

Gorelick, Steve, 116

Gottfried, Martin, 98

Gould, Chester, 80

Gray, Doris, 19

Gray, Harold, 1, 9, 10, 12–14, 19–20, 54–55, 72–73; on Annie, 13–14, 56–57, 65–66, 75–77; biography of, 4, 7–8, 73–75; and "The Crazy Episode," 78; death of, 81, 82; diaries of, 27, 66; during World War II, 46–63; and FDR, 29, 57; and organized labor, 32–35, 64–65, 69–70, 74–75; politics of, 2, 23; and racial issues, 57–58; and rationing board incident, 51–56; success of, 23, 37, 73; Starr on, 105–8

Gray, Winifred Frost, 20, 82

Gray & Gray, 20

Grease (musical), 110

Great Depression, 22

Green, Maw (character), 27

Green, Mitzi, 43

Greenfield, Meg, 97

Greensboro, (N.C.) *Daily News*, 80

Gudge, Uriah (character), 36

Gumps, The (comic strip), 7, 13, 83

Hancock, Sheila, 100

Hanna-Barbera, 89

Hannigan, Miss, 93, 96, 100, 113, 118

Hannigan, Rooster (character), 93, 113

Harper's (magazine), 72

Hartford *Courant*, 78

Hawthorne, Nathaniel, 36

Heenan, Frances, 14

Hellzapoppin' (musical), 97

Hennessey, Dale, 114, 115, 116, 118

Herrmann, Edward, 113

Higgins, George C., Msgr., 70

Holder, Geoffrey, 113, 118

Hood, Claire, 100

Hoover, Herbert, 23, 24

Hoover, J. Edgar, 97

"Hoovervilles," 23

House of the Seven Gables (Hawthorne), 36

Houston *Post*, 79

Humbug Sigel, 40

Huntington (W. Va.) *Herald Dispatch*, 34–35

Hurd, Jud, 73

Huston, John, 110, 116

I Remember Mama (musical), 94

Ignico, Robin, 112, 114

Insull, Samuel J., 29–32, 62

Ivy, Mrs. (character), 61

John, Collar (character), 71

Johns, Strafford, 100

Jones, Jesse, 61

Juliet Jones (comic strip), 84

Junior (character), 69

"Junior Commando" movement, 46–51

Juvenile delinquency, 68–71

Kelly, Walt, 77, 83

Kerr, Walter, 94, 95, 96, 98

Kennedy, Jacqueline, 100

Kennedy Center (Washington, D.C.), 97

King, Frank, 83

King Features Syndicate, 20

Kleiser, Randal, 110

Kolassal, Mr. (character), 44–45

Kurtzman, Harvey, 77

Labor movement, 32, 64–65, 69–70, 74–75
Lafayette (Ind.) *Morning Journal,* 7
"Lament for Annie, A" (Coates), 80
Laro, Arthur, 82
Layton, Joe, 110, 112, 115
"Leapin' Lizards! Has Annie Gone Pinko?!?" (Abel), 99
Lee, Angela, 112
Leffingwell, Robert, 83
LeQuaque, Dr. (character), 78
Lerman, April, 114
"Let's Go to the Movies" (song), 111
Lettick, David, 85, 88
Lewis, John L., 32
L'il Abner (comic strip), 72, 77, 80
L'il Abner (musical), 89
Lindbergh, Charles, 46
Little Annie Fanny (comic strip), 77
Little Annie Rooney (comic strip), 20–21
Little Arf an' Nannie (comic strip), 77
Little Orphan Annie (comic strip): after Gray's death, 83–87, 103; cancellation of, 17, 34, 54–56, 68, 78, 79, 84–85; creation of, 2–3, 6–10; criticism of, 47, 55–56, 62, 63, 64–65, 66, 68, 69, 86; early episodes of, 13–21; and "Fred Flask Flap," 51–56; in the 20's, 13–21; in the 30's, 22–37; in the 40's, 46–63; in the 50's, 68–70; in the 70's, 103; parodies of, 77; plotting of, 27–28; politics in, 2, 31–32, 33–35, 57–58; 62–63, 66–68, 72–73, 105; reader response to, 17–18, 35, 55–56, 60, 61, 66–67, 75, 80, 85; violence in, 68, 69–73
Little Orphan Annie (film; 1932), 23, 43–44
Little Orphan Annie (film; 1938), 23, 44
"Little Orphan Annie" (radio program), 23, 38–43
Little Orphan Asylum Society, 85
"Little Orphan Nannie" (song), 40
Little Orphan Otto (comic strip), 9
"Little Orphant Annie" (Riley poem), 3–4
Loeb, William, 60
London *Illustrated News,* 7
"Lone Ranger, The" (radio program), 42
Long Beach (Cal.) *Independent Press Telegram,* 78–79
Longstreth, George, 73
Loretta (character), 48
Los Angeles *Times,* 67, 78
Loudon, Dorothy, 96, 99
Louisville *Courier-Journal,* 54
Luce, Clare Booth, 56–57

McArdle, Andrea, 90, 97, 99, 100, 111
McClure, Darrell, 21
McCormack, Robert, 7, 54
McCutcheon, John T., 8
McManus, George, 83
McSnoots, Tootsie (character), 44
Mad (magazine), 77
Mansfield (Ohio) *News-Journal,* 62
March, Marvin, 116–117

Marshall Field galleries, 20
Martin, Gary, 115
Mattingly, Ignatius, 72
Meehan, Thomas, 88, 89, 94, 95, 98, 99, 101, 110, 111
Mellon, Andrew W., 32
Michel, Don, 104
Mickey (character), 43
Minami, Roger, 113
Mitchell, David, 96, 99
Monmouth College (N.J.), 114
Moon Mullins (comic strip), 7
Mutt and Jeff (comic strip), 83

NBC Blue Network, 39
Nederlander, James, 92, 96, 99, 100
Neuberger, Richard, 31
New Deal, 29, 34
New Republic, 29, 31, 34–35
New York (magazine), 99
New York *Daily News,* 6, 9, 13, 29, 44, 46, 47, 54, 86, 98, 105
New York *Post,* 98
New York *Times,* 94–95, 98, 101
News Syndicate Co., 54
Nichols, Mike, 95, 97, 99
Northcliffe, Lord, 7

O'Connor, Donald, 111
Office of Price Administration (OPA), 51–55
Ohio State Journal, 70
Oliver! (musical), 90
On Location (magazine), 116
On Stage (comic strip), 83, 103, 104, 106
Oregon Labor Press, 69
Orphan Annie (cocktail), 97
Ovaltine, 38, 40–42
Owens, Del, 39

Panda (character), 48
Paradiso, Robert, 114, 115, 116
Paramount, 44
Parker, Sarah Jessica, 102
Parson, Hubert, 115
Pathe Review, 20
Patterson, Joseph Medill, 7, 8, 9, 13, 16, 17, 54
Peanuts (comic strip), 79
Peg, Old Shanghai (character), 36–37
Perkins, Mary (character), 103
Peters, Bernadette, 90, 113
Pewter, Mrs. (character), 20
Phillips, Arlene, 110, 115
Piffleberry, Selbert Adlebert (character), 17
Playboy (magazine), 77
Pogo (comic strip), 77, 83
Porter, Bobby, 117
Posit, Iziah D. (character), 12
Poston, Gretchen, 97
Powers, David, 97, 100
Premiums, 41

Price, Michael, 92
Prince Valiant (comic strip), 83
Punjab (character), 28, 43, 48, 60, 82, 91, 113

Quinn, Aileen, 112, 118

Radio, "Little Orphan Annie" on, 38–43
Radio City Music Hall, 116
Radio Orphan Annie's "Secret Society," 41
Raduta, Henry, 83
Rastar Films, 44
Rationing, 51
Reed, Robert S., 85, 92, 99, 104
Reilly, Maurice, 69
Reinking, Ann, 113
Reuther, Walter, 32
Riley, James Whitcomb, 3–4
RKO Radio Pictures, 43
Rochester (N.Y.) *Democrat-Chronicle,* 50, 68
Rockledge (Gray estate), 37
Rooney, Annie (character), 20–21
Roosevelt, Eleanor, 58
Roosevelt, Franklin D., 2, 28–29, 57, 63, 93, 96, 99, 113
Root, Herb (character), 12
Ruane, Janine, 93
Ryan, Stephen P., 71

St. Louis *Globe-Democrat,* 70
St. Regis, Lily (character), 113
Samson, Simple (character), 68
Sandy (character), 2, 16, 68, 93, 96, 100, 114
Sandy Kennel Club, 85
Saturday Review, 39
Sawbucks, Daddy (character), 77
Scalpel, Doc (character), 12
Schultz, Charles, 79
Selznick, David O., 43, 112
Setter, Sam (character), 61
Shark, J.J. (character), 26
Shelton, Reid, 93, 94, 96
Siegel, Larry, 40
"Sign" (song), 111
Silo, Mr. & Mrs. (characters), 16, 19, 39
Slott, Mollie, 75
Slugg, J. (character), 33–34
Smith, Allison, 102
Smith, Sidney, 7, 13, 83
Sobieski, Carol, 110, 116
Sorrentino, Rosanne, 114
Spangle, Sally (character), 51, 55
Spangle, Spike (character), 51, 55, 56
Spangles, Janey (character), 44, 45
Stark, Ray, 110, 112
Starr, Leonard, 103–8
Steinbrunner, Chris, 42
Steiner, Max, 43
Stevens, Roger, 96
Stewart, Lucie, 114
Streisand, Barbra, 100, 110

Strouse, Charles, 88, 94, 95, 98, 99, 109, 111
Superman (musical), 90
Syracuse (N.Y.) *Post-Standard,* 70

Talese, Gay, 14
Task, Maggie, 93
Tell, William (character), 12
Thimble, Lawyer (character), 62
Thorne, Raymond, 93, 100
Thy Neighbor's Wife (Talese), 14
Time (magazine), 73, 77–78
"Tomorrow" (song), 91, 101, 102
Tompkins Corners, 39
Torme, Mel, 39
Tort, Judge (character), 12
Toze, Anya (character), 108
Tribune Company Syndicate, 13, 38, 50, 51, 54, 89, 103, 104
Trowel, Old Tom (character), 12
Trudeau, Garry, 57
True, Garrison, 111

U.S. Steel, 32
Union Times (newspaper), 65
Universal Pictures, 96
Updown, Mr. (character), 44–45

Valentines (characters), 69
Variety, 44
Vigard, Kristen, 93, 94
Vlamos, James Frank, 47

Wallace, Minnie McIntyre, 17
Walsh, Brandon, 21
Warbucks, Mrs. (character), 11, 16, 17, 19, 20
Warbucks, Oliver "Daddy" (character), 16, 24–27
Warbucks, 24–25, 27–28, 29, 31, 32, 33, 34, 42, 43, 46–48; in *Annie*, 91, 94, 96, 99; character of, 2–3, 12; death of, 58, 82; Finney as, 112–113; first appearance of, 11–12; resurrection of, 62, 105
Warbucks, Trixie (character), 28
Washington *Post,* 70, 87
Waterbury (Conn.) *Republican-American,* 54
Watt, Douglas, 98
"We've Got Annie" (song), 111
WGN (radio station), 38, 42
Williams, Nick B., 79–80
Wilson, Eileen, 37
Winnie Winkle (comic strip), 77
Witches (characters), 39
Withers, Jane, 111

You're a Good Man, Charlie Brown (play), 89
Young, Chic, 83

Zane, Mr. (character), 48
Zero (character), 21

ABOUT THE AUTHOR

Bruce Smith is a writer and editor at the New York *Daily News*. He grew up in the Midwest and New England and graduated from Marquette University's College of Journalism. He is a member of the New York Press Club and lives in Old Greenwich, Connecticut.